THE BOY IN THE TREEHOUSE

GIRL WHO LOVED HER HORSES

Drew Hayden Taylor

Talonbooks

Talonbooks
278 East First Avenue, Vancouver, British Columbia, Canada, V5T 1A6
www.talonbooks.com

Seventh printing: November 2017

Typeset in New Baskerville
Printed and bound in Canada

Cover design by Adam Swica

Talonbooks gratefully acknowledges the financial support of the Canada Council for the Arts, the Government of Canada through the Canada Book Fund, and the Province of British Columbia through the British Columbia Arts Council and the Book Publishing Tax Credit.

Rights to produce *The Boy in the Treehouse* or *Girl Who Loved Her Horses*, in whole or in part, in any medium by any group, amateur or professional, are retained by the author. Interested persons are requested to contact Janine Cheeseman, Aurora Artists' Management, 19 Wroxeter Avenue, Toronto, Ontario M4K 1J5; tel.: 416-463-4634; fax: 416-463-4889; email: aurora.artists@sympatico.ca.

Library and Archives Canada Cataloguing in Publication

Taylor, Drew Hayden, 1962–
    The boy in the treehouse ; Girl who loved her horses

    Plays.
    ISBN 0-88922-441-2

    I. Title. II. Title: Girl who loved her horses.
PS8589.A885B69 2000   C812'.54   C00910755-X
PR9199.3.T35B69 2000

ISBN-10: 0-88922-441-2
ISBN-13: 978-0-88922-441-4

Contents

Introduction

I find it odd that this, my eleventh book, is a return to my origins in theatre. My very first play (and first book), which appeared over ten years ago, was a tentative little offering about kids called *Toronto at Dreamer's Rock*. It was moderately successful. A lot has happened since then.

The Boy in the Treehouse and *Girl Who Loved Her Horses* once again explore the world of theatre for younger audiences (though adults are more than welcome, if they remember to pack their imaginations). Both plays offer something different to the theatre practitioner and audience member. These plays, each featuring young protagonists, investigate the dilemmas of being not quite understood because of our age. Who among us cannot relate to that?

It seems the journey of youth is one of searching for social acceptance, navigating the minefield of well-meaning parents and trying to figure out how this world works (the latter of which, as a full-blown adult, I am still working at). They say being young is the most wonderful part of your life, but it can also be the most horrible and trying. To quote the opening line of a fabulous book, "It was the best of times. It was the worst of times ..." I don't think it was ever better put.

Girl Who Loved Her Horses is my personal favourite of everything I have ever written. It's one of those cases where every time I read it, I can't believe I wrote it. Some consider it an adult memory play, but at its core, it's a story of a little girl whose imagination is her only friend and the power that such a friend can give. In some unfortunate cases, it's the only thing that keeps us alive. I think we all have a little Danielle in us.

The Boy in the Treehouse is my most recent play. It deals with the dilemma of being from mixed parentage, specifically Native and non-Native, and the issues that involves. In this increasingly multicultural world, it's a matter that will become more and more relevant to our children as the years pass. Add to that the death of a parent and the world truly does become a confusing place for poor Simon.

One play is about a girl. One is about a boy. One takes place on the Reserve, the other in an urban environment. One is about imagination, the other is about visions. One has a happy ending, the other does not. Yet they cover the spectrum of the issues and experiences that our young Native people face every day.

As Simon would say, "You have the best of both worlds." And as Danielle would say, "Thank you."

—DREW HAYDEN TAYLOR

THE BOY IN THE TREEHOUSE

Manitoba Theatre for Young People commissioned *The Boy in the Treehouse*. The play premiered as a co-production with Toronto's Harbourfront Centre in Winnipeg in May 2000, with the following cast:

SIMON: Herbie Barnes
FATHER: Harry Nelken
PATTY, CAMERAMAN: Sharon King
NEIGHBOUR, POLICEMAN,
REPORTER, CLYDE: David Gillies

Directed by Herbie Barnes
Set and costumes by Brian Perchaluk
Composer: Cathy Nosaty
Lighting design by Hugh Conacher
Stage manager: Carolyn Kutchyera

Cast
Simon: A twelve-year-old Native boy
Father: Simon's father, a White man
Patty: An annoying, but smart, girl about the same
   age as Simon
Neighbour / policeman / reporter / Clyde:
   All roles can be played by one adult actor.

Setting
The play takes place in a suburban backyard, with a treehouse, somewhere in Winnipeg (though it could be anywhere).

Time
The present.

Production Notes
It is important to note that the treehouse should be a world unto itself. In fact, the entire tree landscape (including Patty's tree) should be essentially separate from the world of the father and the supporting characters. It should be a different reality up there, perhaps even a spirit world. Consequently, there should be two distinct performing areas, one on the ground and the other in the trees. So, be sure you have sturdy trees (and light actors who have a good sense of balance).

In the Winnipeg production, the audience sat on bleachers that bookended the set. People seated at the top of the bleachers were at the same elevation as Simon and his world. It was a wonderful vantage point from which to view the play.

Although I have been asked if a Native actress should play the character of Patty, I have intentionally left her appearance and cultural background vague. You should make this call as you see fit.

Scene One

The lights come up on a suburban backyard. Dividing the stage are two large trees, one topped with a large treehouse. The treehouse has no railings except for one post attached near a corner. At one end of the stage is the rear entrance to a house. A solemn young boy exits the house carrying a duffle bag. His name is SIMON and he is of mixed Native and White ancestry. He walks toward the treehouse like he has a mission. He stops at the bottom of the tree, fortifies himself with a big breath and climbs up a ladder to the treehouse. Once inside, he pulls the ladder up into the tree, staying noticeably clear of the edge. He is cut off from the earth. SIMON is clearly uncomfortable with his elevation. Grasping the pole tightly, he surveys his domain.

SIMON
    So far, so good.

Lights down.

Scene Two

SIMON is sitting on the floor in the centre of the treehouse, well away from the edge. He is sorting stuff from his duffle bag. There are some clothes, several books, a blanket, a bottle of water and a Walkman. As he prepares his treehouse, SIMON's FATHER enters, coming home from work.

SIMON
    Hey, Dad.

FATHER
    What? Oh hi, Simon. What are you doing up there?

SIMON
    Getting ready for a vision quest.

FATHER
    That's nice. Be sure you're done by dinnertime.

SIMON
    Uh, Dad, it's a vision quest.

FATHER
    I heard you. Have fun. Dinner will still be at seven, like always.

SIMON
    Dad, do you know what a vision quest is?

FATHER
A video game?

SIMON
How could you live with Mom all those years
and not know what a vision quest is?

FATHER
What's your mother got to do with this?

SIMON
Never mind, it's a Native thing. I don't want
dinner.

FATHER
A Native thing, huh? Well, I happen to know
from personal experience, and, contrary to
what you seem to believe, Native people *do* eat.
Most of them eat at dinnertime, too. And I
knew your mother and her family longer than
you. And I've seen them eat. So obviously I
know more about what you're talking about
than you do. Got ya. How do you feel about
chicken tonight?

SIMON
I don't want dinner. I can't eat.

FATHER
Aren't you feeling well?

SIMON
No, Dad, you don't understand. I'm getting
ready for a vision quest. It's not a video game or

anything like that. It's called a ritual. Native
people do it all the time.

FATHER
And it involves sitting in trees and not having
dinner? Simon, I don't remember your mother
doing that.

SIMON
Only boys do it. It's part of becoming a man.

FATHER
(*smiling to himself*) Oh, I see. A man, huh? Okay,
then. You want to miss dinner, that's your
business. If you change your mind, dinner's at
seven.

SIMON
Thank you.

FATHER
How long will this "becoming a man" thing
take?

SIMON
It depends. Could be days.

FATHER
You're not planning to eat for a couple of days!

SIMON
Yep. It's called fasting.

FATHER
Simon, that may not be healthy.

SIMON
Monks and people like that all over the world
fast all the time.

FATHER
Are you a monk now, too?

SIMON
I told you, it's a Native thing. You wouldn't
understand. I'll be okay. I'll let you know if I
need anything. Okay, Dad?

FATHER
(*unsure*) Yeah, okay.

> *SIMON continues fiddling about in the treehouse
> while the FATHER, unconvinced and a little
> worried, slowly enters the house. He's inside for
> less than a few seconds before he comes rushing
> out again.*

FATHER
Simon, I'm not sure if I like this. Maybe you
should come down now. You've never been that
comfortable up there. That's why we never got
around to finishing it.

SIMON
I'll be okay; I've read all about this kind of
thing.

> *SIMON holds up a couple of books.*

SIMON
See. They tell me everything I need to know.

FATHER
Simon ...

SIMON
Dad, I have to do this.

FATHER
But why? I know this is a "Native thing," but
could you at least try to explain this to your
poor, White father? Why do you have to starve
yourself up in a tree?

SIMON
I'm doing it for Mom.

FATHER
Oh, Simon, I don't think your mother would
want you to do something like this. In fact I'm
sure of it. So why don't you be a good boy
and—

SIMON
I told you you wouldn't understand. Mom was
Native; you're not. I'm somewhere in the
middle.

FATHER
Is that what this is about?

SIMON
Kind of. Sort of. Maybe. I'm not sure. All I
know is I have to do this, for Mom's sake. And
for mine. It's important.

> *The FATHER is silent for a moment, seeing the
> pain in his son's eyes.*

FATHER
What does all this involve? Other than starving
and sitting in a tree.

SIMON
I have to be by myself.

FATHER
By yourself.

SIMON
Alone. You know, so I don't get distracted.

FATHER
Is that your way of asking me to go away?

SIMON
It's part of the ritual.

FATHER
Part of the ritual. I see. Okay.

The FATHER turns to leave.

FATHER
I'll be inside.

SIMON
I know.

*The FATHER reluctantly enters the house. He is
a concerned man. SIMON picks up one of the
books, opens it to a page and studies for a
moment. He then positions himself in the centre
of the treehouse, facing the audience. He is cross-
legged and has his arms sitting on his lap. He*

checks the book again, making sure he's got the position correct. Putting the book down, he begins to drum his hand on the floor of the treehouse. He follows a steady rhythm for a moment, then loses it. He tries again and the same thing happens. Then he opens his eyes, frustrated.

SIMON
    Well, that's boring.

Scene Three

SIMON wakes up from a nap to find one of his arms and part of his leg dangling over the edge of the treehouse. Panicking, he rolls to the centre. Now fully awake, he picks up a bottle of water. Before he can take a drink, there is a voice behind him in the other tree.

PATTY
Can I have a drink?

SIMON lets out a scream of surprise, spraying the water.

SIMON
Where'd you come from?

PATTY
Near Brandon. Why? You got relatives there?

SIMON
You scared ... I mean surprised me.

PATTY
Sorry. I just saw you sitting up here earlier, talking to that guy. You got me curious. Whatcha doin' up here?

SIMON
You wouldn't understand.

PATTY
    I watch a lot of television. I understand plenty.
    Pretty cool treehouse. You make it yourself?

SIMON
    Yeah, me and my dad.

PATTY
    Was that him?

SIMON
    Yeah.

PATTY
    I always wanted one like this. Except maybe
    with railings. And a roof. But this one is pretty
    okay. I live over that way. Just moved. All we
    got's a few skinny cedars in our backyard. Only
    thing they'll hold is a couple of bird feeders.
    No fun. You're lucky.

SIMON
    Who are you?

PATTY
    My name's Patty. Hi.

SIMON
    Hi. I'm Simon.

PATTY
    Hi, Simon. Can I have a drink then?

SIMON
    Uh, sure, I guess.

PATTY makes her way through the trees to the
treehouse. She takes the bottle and drinks.

PATTY
Thanks. Was gettin' kind of thirsty and didn't
have any money on me to buy a drink. You
know how it is. Anyways, I was checking out the
neighbourhood, you know, gettin' familiar. New
kid on the block and all that. Saw that tree
there, apple tree. Love wild apples. The store-
bought Macs haven't any taste to them. I like
something that bites back. Know what I mean?

SIMON
Yeah, I guess.

PATTY
My mother makes a mean apple pie. That's
where I get my fondness for apples. She prefers
to use wild apples, when she can get them. You
haven't lived till you've had my mom's apple
pie. Maybe you can come over and have some
sometime.

SIMON
Uh, sure.

PATTY
So, like, I was out seeing if I could find some.
You know, for my mom and her pies. It's kind
of hard finding good apple trees in the city,
with all the houses and all. Then I saw that one.
Unfortunately, that tree looks like it's between
seasons. Did you know that? Apple trees, at least
wild ones, only make apples every other year. I

guess this one is between them. Too bad, looks
like it might have some good ones. Hey, you
eaten any from that tree?

SIMON
Uh, yeah … look …

PATTY
Are they any good? I mean, do they have a bite?
Something my mother might like? Or does your
mother use them? They also make good jams
and applesauce. Are there any other apple trees
around here?

SIMON
My mother planted those small ones over there
when I was born.

PATTY
Hey, I don't want to take them if your mom's
got rights on them first. Don't want to start any
trouble, if you know what I mean. Your
neighbourhood and all.

SIMON
Um, yes. No. Uh, I mean … take them. Go
ahead. We don't use them.

PATTY
No?! Too bad. You don't know what you're
missing. Maybe my mom can give your mom
her pie recipe. What do ya think? People would
die for it.

SIMON
My mother's dead.

PATTY
Oh. (*pause*) Sorry. I do things like that. My
father once said I took up all the oxygen in a
room just asking stupid questions. Good thing
I'm in a tree, huh, lots of oxygen up here. So
just you and your father, huh?

SIMON
Yeah.

PATTY
So what are you doing up here? Just hanging
out?

SIMON
I want to have a vision quest.

PATTY
Cool. Can I, too?

SIMON
No. You're supposed to do it alone. And
besides, it's only for boys.

PATTY
Well, excuse me. If only boys do it, then it must
be stupid. Why just boys?

SIMON
I don't know. It just is.

PATTY

As my father says, nothing "just is." There's got to be a reason. I'll bet you just don't know it. And I doubt if it has a good reason, too. I mean, you're just sitting here, not doing anything. Like that takes a lot of brains.

SIMON

Do you mind?! This is *my* treehouse.

PATTY

I know. Look, there's a nail sticking out. You might want to hammer it in deeper before you or somebody else trips on it. It's a long way down. I doubt you're insured. Did I tell you my uncle sells insurance? But I don't know if they have it for treehouses. They should, don't you think? So what's a vision quest?

SIMON

I forget … I mean … it's a ritual.

PATTY

Oh, that tells me a lot. What kind of ritual? Not something weird, is it?

SIMON

No. It's very ancient, very old. It's when boys would go off to some high, quiet place to be by themselves. And that means alone. No one else around. They're supposed to chant and pray and do stuff like that for a couple days.

PATTY
  Why?

SIMON
  To have a vision.

PATTY
  What kind of vision? A television?

SIMON
  Don't be silly. Different kinds of visions.

PATTY
  Like I said, you don't know, do you?

SIMON
  I do, too.

PATTY
  Then what kind of vision are you supposed to
  have?

SIMON
  It depends what you're looking for.

PATTY
  Then what are you looking for, huh?

SIMON
  None of your business.

PATTY
  See, I told you you don't know.

SIMON
  It has to do with my mother, okay?

PATTY
What about your mother?

SIMON
Look, I know where there are some apple trees, ones that have apples on them.

PATTY
You do? Where?

SIMON
Two blocks down, there's a park. On the other side of the park is a small stream. There are two apple trees on both sides of the stream.

PATTY
Excellent. Are the apples any good?

SIMON
They're great. Wonderful. Amazing. But you better hurry, they're almost all gone or on the ground.

PATTY
Cool. Thanks. I'll go check it out.

SIMON
You do that.

PATTY climbs into the other tree.

PATTY
Oh, by the way, good luck with your chanting and praying and stuff. Bye.

PATTY disappears. SIMON gets back into position, then notices:

SIMON
  She took my water!

Scene Four

*It is evening. A faint chanting can be heard
coming from the treehouse. SIMON can't be seen
in the darkness. The next-door NEIGHBOUR is
outside barbecuing. He is puzzled by the
chanting. The FATHER comes out and sees the
NEIGHBOUR looking at the treehouse. He begins
raking the lawn in an attempt to be
inconspicuous.*

NEIGHBOUR
Hey, how're ya doing there, Tom? That your
boy I hear?

FATHER
Yes.

NEIGHBOUR
Got a nice voice. What's he doing?

FATHER
I think it's called chanting.

NEIGHBOUR
Chanting, huh? It's good the boy has a hobby.
Want a burger?

FATHER
No, thank you, Stanley. I ate already.

NEIGHBOUR
Too bad. They're good. Made them myself. The
secret's in mixing the meat with dried onion
soup mix. Gives them a real kick. Maybe your
boy would like one.

FATHER
I hope he does. He must be pretty hungry by
now.

NEIGHBOUR
Boys do love their treehouses, don't they? I
used to spend hours in mine. I almost never
came down. (*pause*) I don't remember doing
much chanting, though. Must be one of those
new trendy things kids are interested in.

FATHER
Actually, it's supposed to be quite old. He says
he's doing some Native thing. I think he misses
his mother.

A silence settles on the backyard.

NEIGHBOUR
It was hard on the boy, wasn't it?

FATHER
But he never cried. Simon never cried at the
funeral.

NEIGHBOUR
I'm not too fond of boys crying, but you'd think
they would when their own mother passes away.
Can't fault them for that.

FATHER
He wouldn't let himself.

NEIGHBOUR
That's not the kind of thing you'd think they'd "let" happen. It just does. I was twice as old as Simon when my mother went, I'm not ashamed to say my eyes were a little wet.

FATHER
Simon likes to be in control.

NEIGHBOUR
Is that good for a boy that young?

FATHER
I don't know. I hope he's okay.

NEIGHBOUR
Look, he's a good kid. Maybe it's just a phase he's going through or something. My kids have had so many phases, I don't recognize them from day to day. You know, Tania has green hair now?! She looks like a Christmas decoration. Here.

The NEIGHBOUR quickly puts a hamburger patty in a bun and wraps it up. He hands it to the FATHER.

NEIGHBOUR
Give this to Simon. He loves my hamburgers. So did his mother. Maybe it will put him in a good mood. Tell him it's from Stan the Hamburger Man.

FATHER
He'll appreciate it. He must be hungry. This just might be the bait I need to get him down. Thanks.

NEIGHBOUR
And, Tom, tell him it's okay to cry.

The FATHER walks toward the treehouse and the NEIGHBOUR exits.

FATHER
Hey, Simon, you still up there?

SIMON appears.

SIMON
I thought I heard you. (*sniffs*) Is that Mr. Manley's barbecue I smell?

FATHER
Yes, I have a hamburger ...

SIMON
Dad, you know I have to fast. And fasting means no food.

FATHER
But you don't want to hurt Mr. Manley's feelings, do you? One little hamburger.

SIMON
Dad!

FATHER
Okay, okay, you can't blame a father for trying.
You going to be okay up there? I mean, it might
get kind of cold tonight. You want a blanket or
something? That's not against the rules, is it?

SIMON
Don't worry, Dad, I got everything I need. I
came prepared.

FATHER
Very smart of you.

SIMON
That hamburger does smell good. Is it the one
with the onion soup in it?

FATHER
That's what he said.

SIMON
Those are so good.

> *SIMON is wavering. His eyes are fixed on the
> wrapped hamburger.*

SIMON
But I can't.

> *He quickly disappears back into the treehouse.
> There is silence. The FATHER waits for a minute
> or two.*

FATHER
(*to himself*) And I'm to tell you it is okay to cry.

The FATHER exits.

Scene Five

SIMON is sitting cross-legged with his Walkman on. His eyes are closed. PATTY appears in the nearby tree and makes her way to the treehouse.

PATTY
Hey, Simon, you still up there?

SIMON can't hear her. She climbs into the treehouse, carrying a half-full bag and his water bottle.

PATTY
Simon!

PATTY touches SIMON on the shoulder and he reacts, startled. She jumps back, startled, too.

SIMON
Will you quit doing that!

PATTY
I yelled but you didn't hear me. What are you listening to?

SIMON
Stuff.

PATTY
Tell me.

SIMON
It's my Walkman.

PATTY
Is it some sort of weird music or something? Let
me hear.

*She quickly grabs the Walkman and, before
SIMON can get it off her, she has it switched on
and is listening to it. SIMON tries to get it back
but realizes it's futile. He stops. A puzzled look
appears on PATTY's face.*

PATTY
I hear loons. And frogs. Crickets, too. That's
one weird band.

SIMON
It's not a band; it's called a nature tape. It plays
all sorts of nature sounds to create what they
call "an atmosphere."

PATTY
You're in a treehouse. What do you need
"atmosphere" for?

SIMON
For my vision quest. And what are you doing
here anyways? I thought you went off apple
hunting.

PATTY
I did. And look: (*holds up the bag*) success! I
wanted to share them with you; after all, it was
your suggestion. How many do you want?

SIMON

I don't want any. Look, I'm trying to be alone
here so I can fast. Everybody keeps stopping by
and offering me food. I can't concentrate.

PATTY

Well, sorry. If this vision quest thing of yours is
supposed to make you grumpy and mean,
you're doing good. How long do you plan to be
up here anyways?

SIMON

I don't know. It's different for different people.
It's a spiritual thing. Probably a couple of days.
Until I have my vision.

PATTY

I see. Maybe glasses would help.

SIMON

What?!

PATTY

They're supposed to help with vision, aren't
they?

SIMON

Grrrr …

PATTY

A couple of days, huh? And you're gonna stay
up here the whole time?

SIMON

Yes.

PATTY
Where are you going to go to the bathroom?

This is a thought that had escaped SIMON. He looks around the treehouse with sudden realization.

PATTY
Or does part of this vision quest thing mean you don't go to the bathroom?

PATTY playfully squirts water out of the water bottle, teasing SIMON until he takes it away from her. He suddenly becomes embarrassed over his bathroom situation.

PATTY
In fact, you've been up here almost half a day now, haven't you? Boy, I'm surprised you ain't had to go by now. Oh well, that's your business. Try not to think about it. That only makes it worse. A little something I picked up on bus trips. Anyways, sorry you don't want the apples, but have fun. Bye.

PATTY exits the treehouse, leaving behind a worried and concerned SIMON.

SIMON
Oh geez …

SIMON glances nervously over the side of the treehouse.

Scene Six

It is early morning. The stage is empty. A
POLICEMAN enters, casually looking around,
then approaches the treehouse. Looking up, the
POLICEMAN tries to peer into its shadows.
Finding nothing interesting, the POLICEMAN
approaches the back door and knocks. The
FATHER answers, dressed in a bathrobe.

FATHER
Officer, is something wrong?

POLICEMAN
Good morning, sir. Sorry to bother you so early,
but we've had reports of unusual noises back
here. I'm here to check it out.

FATHER
They came from back here?

POLICEMAN
This may sound strange, but, according to the
reports, it's up in the trees. We've already called
the zoo to see if they've had any monkeys
escape, but no luck. Hey, don't laugh, it's
happened. South American howler monkey
once got out of its cage a couple of years ago,
ran amok in a park for a week. Poor thing
couldn't find anything to eat other than a few
insects.

FATHER
I'm sorry, but to the best of my knowledge,
there are no monkeys in my backyard. (*SIMON
drops a book.*) Unless you count my son. He's up
in the treehouse.

POLICEMAN
Mind if I have a chat with him?

FATHER
He may not like it.

POLICEMAN
Doesn't like cops?

FATHER
He's got some silly idea in his head about
staying up there until he has a vision.

POLICEMAN
A vision? What kind of vision?

FATHER
He won't say. But he says he's not coming down
until he has one. I suppose I could go up there
and drag him down, but that might just make
things worse.

POLICEMAN
I'll have a word with him. What's his name?

FATHER
Simon.

POLICEMAN
Had an uncle named Simon. He was nuts.

The POLICEMAN moves to the treehouse.

POLICEMAN
Simon! Could I talk to you a moment?

SIMON appears, puzzled. It's obvious he'd been sleeping.

SIMON
What's going on?

POLICEMAN
Just want to ask you a few questions. Can you come down here for a few minutes?

SIMON
Um, Dad ...

FATHER
Officer, he's up there doing some sort of ritual. It's important for him to stay where he is. Can you talk to him while he's up there?

POLICEMAN
Uh-huh. A ritual, huh?

FATHER
It doesn't involve monkeys or anything, just himself.

POLICEMAN
Sure. Okay, Simon, some people have complained that they've seen and heard somebody or something moving around up here last night. Do you know anything about it?

SIMON
No. I've been in here all night. I haven't
moved. Maybe it was Patty. She was up here for
a little bit last night. She sure talks a lot. I can
see why people would complain about her.

FATHER
Who's Patty?

SIMON
Some girl that's new in the neighbourhood.
Said she was looking for apples for her
mother's apple pie. She was here twice
yesterday, including last night.

FATHER
I didn't see her.

SIMON
She came up through that tree and crossed
over to here.

POLICEMAN
Was this girl's father Tarzan?

SIMON
No, seriously, she wouldn't leave me alone.

FATHER
She walked from there … to there?!

SIMON
Yes.

> *The POLICEMAN and the FATHER look at each*
> *other for a moment. SIMON notices this and*
> *reacts indignantly.*

SIMON
 She did!

POLICEMAN
 How long are you going to be up there, son?

SIMON
 I don't know. As long as it takes.

POLICEMAN
 You got your father all worried. You should
 forget all this apples-and-Patty nonsense and
 come down now, before you hurt yourself.

SIMON
 I'm not hurting myself.

POLICEMAN
 You could get dizzy and fall out of that thing if
 you're not careful. I've seen it happen.

SIMON
 I won't fall.

POLICEMAN
 A word of advice, kid: stay up there too long,
 and Social Services will come and get you
 down. Do you want that? I mean, if they think
 you're up here doing yourself no good, they'll
 be up there quicker than a squirrel after a nut.
 And they'll blame your father. Maybe take him

to court. They will, you know? Do you want
that, too?

SIMON
No, sir.

POLICEMAN
You think about that as you sit up there. Is what
you're doing worth all that? Think about it.

SIMON disappears back into the treehouse.

POLICEMAN
Maybe that will put the fear of God into him.

FATHER
My son's going through a difficult time at the
moment.

POLICEMAN
If he starts seeing any more people climbing
through these trees, you might consider getting
him some help.

FATHER
I will, officer. Thank you.

POLICEMAN
My uncle was just the same way.

*The POLICEMAN exits, leaving the worried
FATHER behind.*

SIMON
Dad? You won't let them take me away, will you?

FATHER
Of course not. Uh, about this Patty ... are you
sure you didn't dream her?

SIMON
No. She lives around here, just a few blocks
away, she said. Go look for her if you don't
believe me.

FATHER
Simon, there must be fifty or sixty houses within
a three-block radius.

SIMON
Look for one with skinny cedar trees.

The FATHER looks at SIMON with worry.

SIMON
I'm not making it up. She came from over that
direction.

FATHER
I don't mean to doubt you, but that branch
doesn't look like it could hold anyone ...

SIMON
Look, I'll show you.

*SIMON gets up and goes to the edge of the
treehouse.*

FATHER
Simon, don't.

SIMON
She came from over here.

*As SIMON tries to re-create PATTY's footsteps,
the branch breaks and he almost falls. The
FATHER rushes underneath him, ready to catch
him, but SIMON saves himself.*

FATHER
Simon!

SIMON
I'm okay, Dad, my foot slipped.

FATHER
I'm coming up there. Unhook that ladder.

SIMON
I won't do that again. I promise.

FATHER
At least let me help you, son.

SIMON
I have to do this alone, Dad. Trust me.

FATHER
Okay. You can do this if you want, at least for
tonight. I can't force you to eat, but, Simon, I'm
telling you this right here and now, the minute
I think you're in trouble, it's over. And I mean
over. Do I make myself clear?

SIMON
Yes, Dad. I'm sorry I scared you.

Unconvinced, the FATHER walks away slowly,
glancing back at his son occasionally. Once the
FATHER's gone, SIMON tentatively steps on
PATTY's branch, finding it unsound again.

SIMON
This whole thing is getting weirder and weirder.

Scene Seven

SIMON is trying to get comfortable, but is having difficulty. He's hungry, dirty, tired and so far unsuccessful with his vision quest.

SIMON
Okay, this time.

As he gets himself into position, he hears a voice.

PATTY
So, how's your vision quest going?

PATTY enters the treehouse.

SIMON
How do you do that?

PATTY
Do what?

SIMON
Get over here from over there? I tried it and I almost killed myself.

PATTY
Easy, I got girl bones. They're lighter. So whatcha doin'?

SIMON
 You almost got me in trouble. Some policeman
 was talkin' about us making noise here last
 night. They wouldn't believe me when I told
 them about you.

PATTY
 Oh well, that's their problem. A lot of times my
 parents don't believe me when I tell them
 things. So, any luck with that vision quest thing
 of yours? Doesn't look it. I had a good night's
 sleep last night and had lots and lots of dreams.

SIMON
 I want a vision, not a dream.

PATTY
 What's the difference?

SIMON
 One's supposed to be from the Creator and the
 other's from, I don't know, scary movies.

PATTY
 Why is this so important to you?

SIMON
 Because it is.

PATTY
 Because? That's not a reason. A reason is a
 conscious decision to do something based on
 need or requirements arising from a situation.

 SIMON looks at her.

SIMON
Huh?

PATTY
I read books, too. I almost know what it means.
So what's your reason?

SIMON
It's personal.

PATTY
Even better.

SIMON
Don't you have a life somewhere?

PATTY
Life is wherever I am. Kinda deep, huh? So why
are you waiting for God to contact you? That
could be a long wait and winter's in a couple of
months.

SIMON
I told you, it's a Native thing.

PATTY
Hey, take it easy. Just trying to understand.
Don't you get lonely up here?

SIMON
How? I'm never alone.

PATTY
I would. I'd miss my family if I stayed up in
something like this for very long.

PATTY spots SIMON's duffle bag and pulls a framed photograph out of it.

PATTY
 Who's this?

SIMON
 Give that back.

PATTY
 Is this your mother?

SIMON
 Put it down!

PATTY
 Wow, she looks really Native. Almost Asian.

SIMON grabs it from her and puts it back in his bag.

SIMON
 She's Ojibway.

PATTY
 She's pretty.

SIMON
 I know.

PATTY
 Is she why you're doing this?

SIMON
 None of your business.

PATTY

I get it now. You're doing this vision quest thing
to get a vision from this Creator, hoping to see
your mom. That's weird.

SIMON

No, it's not. And that's not what I'm doing. And
why do you want to know anyways?

PATTY

'Cause I'm curious why you'd want to do
something you don't know much about.

SIMON

I do, too.

PATTY

I know enough to know that you have no idea
what you're doing.

SIMON

I have books.

PATTY

Big deal. My father's read a mountain of books,
but he can't even change a tire on our car. He
knows about things, but he doesn't know
things. I know that sounds strange, but it's true.
You can only get so much from books. Do you
know anything about being Native?

SIMON

Yeah.

PATTY

What?

SIMON
Enough.

PATTY
Oh, that tells me a lot. You don't know
anything, do you?

SIMON
I know all the major aboriginal nations across
Canada.

PATTY
Book.

SIMON
I know all the major Chiefs from the last 150
years.

PATTY
Book.

SIMON
I know how to make pemmican. Do you know
what that is? It's a combination of dried buffalo
meat and berries.

PATTY
Where'd you learn that?

SIMON
(*quietly*) I read it.

PATTY
I win.

> *PATTY gets ready to leave.*

SIMON
So, you're saying I'm just wasting my time up
here?

PATTY
I'm not saying anything. Just that ... I won. Bye.

PATTY disappears.

SIMON
I know what I'm doing. Really, I do.

SIMON's stomach growls.

SIMON
I do.

Scene Eight

The backyard is deserted, but nearby noise and conversation can be heard.

FATHER
I don't think this is right. You might upset him.

The FATHER is practically being pushed into his backyard by a news REPORTER. THE FATHER is trying to discourage him.

FATHER
Just leave the boy alone. He's not doing anything.

REPORTER
Not doing anything! Are you serious! A boy climbs up into his treehouse and says he's never coming down. Now that's a story.

FATHER
He never said that!

REPORTER
Close enough. And this has to do with his mother, right?

FATHER
How did you hear about this anyway?

REPORTER
I'm not at liberty to disclose my sources. Is that
the treehouse? How do we get up there?

FATHER
You don't. He wants to be left alone.

REPORTER
They all want to be left alone. Okay, we can do
it from here. You got a good angle on me,
Dwayne? Dwayne?

*The CAMERAMAN comes running in and takes
position with his camera.*

REPORTER
(*to the FATHER*) Get ready. Here's your fifteen
minutes of fame. Okay, Dwayne, three, two
one ... (*pause*) We are here at the suburban
home of ...

He looks to the FATHER.

FATHER
Whitney.

REPORTER
... Whitney home, where young ...?

FATHER
Simon.

REPORTER
... Simon has retreated into his treehouse for
reasons as yet unknown. Mr. Whitney, how
would you describe your son?

FATHER
Um … he's a very good boy, I guess. Smart, a
little impulsive.

REPORTER
I see. And as his father, what do you suppose
drove young Simon away from this beautiful
home and a comfortable bed, into the branches
and boards of that treehouse? Personal
problems, perhaps?

FATHER
Whatever the reason, it's Simon's reason. And I
think we should honour that.

REPORTER
May we have a word with the young boy at the
heart of this story?

FATHER
He wants to be left alone.

REPORTER
It'll only take a minute.

> *The REPORTER and CAMERAMAN approach
> the tree.*

REPORTER
Simon! Simon Whitney! Are you up there?

> *SIMON appears, puzzled.*

SIMON
Who … who are you?

REPORTER
    CKRZ Television.

FATHER
    I tried to stop them.

REPORTER
    Simon, could you tell us why you are up there
    in that treehouse? And speak loudly, please.

SIMON
    Because.

    There is an awkward silence.

REPORTER
    Because ... what?

SIMON
    Because I want to. Why are you standing in our
    backyard? Because you want to.

REPORTER
    I see. Is this some sort of Native interpretation
    of reality?

SIMON
    Um ... okay ...?

REPORTER
    So, what does your mother's culture offer you
    that your father's doesn't?

SIMON
    I don't understand.

REPORTER
You have embraced your aboriginal heritage.
Obviously, it means more to you than your
father's culture.

SIMON
I … I don't think my father has a culture. Do
you, Dad?

The FATHER is surprised by SIMON's statement.

REPORTER
How does this make you feel, Mr. Whitney?

FATHER
I support my son in his decision to explore his
Native half, but he should also be equally proud
of his non-Native half.

REPORTER
Which would be …?

FATHER
Mostly British.

SIMON
I didn't know that.

FATHER
I thought I had told you.

REPORTER
One more question. What will it take to bring
you back down to earth? What will have to be
done?

There is a silent pause.

SIMON
I'll know when I find it. Now leave me alone!

FATHER
All right. You got what you came for. I would appreciate it if you would kindly get off our property.

REPORTER
Gotta do the extro first. Dwayne, ready?

Again, the CAMERAMAN nods with the camera.

REPORTER
So, as we leave young Simon in his treehouse, on day ... (*to the FATHER*) How long has he been up there altogether?

FATHER
One day.

REPORTER
One day! That's all. (*back to the CAMERAMAN*) So, as we leave young Simon in his treehouse, on day ... one of his vigil, one can't help wondering what this young man will find at the end of his journey. However long it may last? And now back to the studio. (*pause*) That's a wrap. Thanks a lot, Mr. Whitney. If he's still up there, say, next week, give us a call.

FATHER
I don't think so. Goodbye.

REPORTER
> You heard the man, Dwayne. There's a guy
> downtown who eats worms. He says they're
> delicious and nutritious and, get this, he also
> runs a noodle restaurant. Now that's news.

> *The REPORTER and the CAMERAMAN exit.*
> *The FATHER walks over to SIMON.*

FATHER
> How are you doing up there?

SIMON
> It's not as easy as I thought. I'm real hungry.

FATHER
> You can quit anytime, you know. And nobody
> will think the worse of you.

SIMON
> I know. Dad, you don't think I'm, like, ashamed
> or anything about you, or being White or
> anything like that?

FATHER
> Then you'd have to be a little ashamed of
> yourself, too.

SIMON
> And I'm not. Sometimes I do wonder about it,
> me being half-White or Indian, but I never let it
> get to me. I like to think I have the best of both
> worlds.

FATHER
That's a good attitude. Mom would have been proud.

SIMON
I miss Mom. That's why I have to do this.

FATHER
So do I. Do you want to talk about it? I know today is the anniversary of Mom's death. It hurts me as much as it hurts you, but I'm not starving myself up in a tree.

SIMON
Dad, you're not Native. She was.

FATHER
You keep saying that, but this has nothing to do with being Native. I know her family and I've met a lot of other Native people over the years, and none of them have done this.

SIMON
This is different. This has been on my mind for months. And unless I do this, it will continue to stay there and drive me crazy.

FATHER
If this starvation thing doesn't first.

SIMON
Do you remember that song Mom used to sing me when I was a lot younger? You know, to put me to sleep?

FATHER
No. That was her special time with you. I always
let her put you to bed. Do you remember the
song?

SIMON
No, I don't. Not anymore. But I want to. That's
the problem.

They are both quiet for a moment.

SIMON
She used to tell me stories of her growing up
on the Reserve, things her mother told her, all
the funny and weird things that would go on
there.

FATHER
And she told you about this vision quest?

SIMON
No. I learned about it myself. But I'm hoping it
might help me remember her more. She's
slipping away, Dad, in my memory and I don't
want her to. The vision quest is supposed to
help you find your future, but how can you find
your future if you're forgetting your past?

FATHER
You'll always have your mother, and you'll
always have me, and I have a past, too. We can
both share it.

SIMON

Dad, if half of this tree was taken away, do you think it would be able to stand? I have to work this out my way. Okay?

FATHER

I'm just so tempted to get a ladder and climb up there, throw you over my shoulder and take you inside.

SIMON

But you won't.

FATHER

But I won't. Yet. But I can't let this continue much longer. Come sundown tomorrow, regardless of where you are in this vision quest thing, you're coming down. This is what your mother would have wanted, too. Tomorrow, Simon. Good night.

The FATHER retreats into the house. SIMON retreats into the treehouse.

Scene Nine

*It is later that evening. It is dark. SIMON is
sitting at the centre of his treehouse with his
Walkman on. He tears it off in frustration.*

SIMON
Nothing's happening! Why isn't it coming?
(*yelling*) Give me my vision!

*As if to answer him, a twig flies out from the tree
and hits him. He looks up nervously.*

SIMON
Who's there?

PATTY
Three guesses. I saw you on the TV tonight.

SIMON
I don't care. (*pause*) How'd I look?

PATTY
Okay, I guess.

SIMON
I can barely see you. What are you doing way
over there?

PATTY
You don't want me in your treehouse,
remember? "It's a ritual," you said.

SIMON
So, what are you doing here then?

PATTY
I didn't realize how serious you were about this
whole thing. I thought it was just some silly boy
thing. Like football. I can't understand why
boys find football so interesting. How old were
you when your mother died?

SIMON
Old enough to remember her, but young
enough to want to remember more.

PATTY
And she was Native? So that makes you half-
Native. Do you feel half-Native?

SIMON
It's none of your business.

PATTY
Oh, somebody's in a nasty mood. See what a
day without going to the bathroom will do to
you?

SIMON
I'm not nasty. Do I look Native to you?

PATTY
You look kinda Native to me. But I think the
important question is with all these books you
got, do you feel Native?

SIMON

I don't know what I feel. I mean, I always
thought I looked more like my mother than I
do my father, but I really don't know that much
about being Native. But I try. I read a lot of
books about it. You were right about that. But
most of my mother's family live far away. So I
have to do what I can by myself.

PATTY

Can I come over? I don't want to interrupt or
anything, but this branch is kind of hurting my
bum.

SIMON

Nice of you to ask this time.

PATTY

Thanks.

> *PATTY makes her way into the treehouse.*

PATTY

I have a question. How is this going to help you
… I don't know … remember your mother?
That's the part I don't get.

SIMON

In one of the books I read, it says that a vision
quest was supposed to give you a direction in
life, or provide you with guidance, through a
vision. Those were the words they used.

> *PATTY absentmindedly picks up the book and
> leafs through it.*

SIMON
Today is the anniversary of my mother's death.
I wanted to try and remember her, stronger,
better, as sort of my present to her. And to
myself, I guess. There, you happy?

PATTY
It was just a question.

They both hear a slight grumbling.

PATTY
What's that?

SIMON
What?

PATTY
Listen ... there ...

SIMON
That's my stomach.

PATTY
You got a dog in there or something?

SIMON
It goes away.

PATTY
It says here in this book, you're supposed to,
like, go into some sort of training for this,
under the supervision of an Elder. It says it's
kind of important.

SIMON
I know. But I don't have any Elders.

PATTY
Your father's kind of old. Won't he do?

SIMON
It's different. He's not Native, and he doesn't know the right stuff.

PATTY
And you do?

SIMON
Yes.

PATTY
No, you don't. Let me guess, things aren't going the way you expected, are they? Nothing's happening except you're getting hungrier and hungrier. Am I right? The only thing you've seen up here has been me.

SIMON
Give me my book back.

SIMON tries to grab the book.

PATTY
I'm not done with it yet. Let go.

They wrestle with it for a moment.

SIMON
Give it to me!

PATTY
> Don't be so rough.

>> *PATTY's foot accidentally goes off the edge of the treehouse and she slips. She almost falls out of the treehouse, but SIMON manages to grab her and, after a scary moment, pulls her to safety. They both realize what almost happened.*

SIMON
> You okay?

>> *PATTY hits him with the book.*

PATTY
> You stupid … jerk … boy! You almost got me killed!

SIMON
> I'm sorry. I didn't mean to …

PATTY
> Keep your stupid book.

>> *PATTY gets up to leave.*

PATTY
> If you wanted me to leave, you could have just told me. You didn't have try and throw me from this stupid treehouse.

SIMON
> It was an accident. I didn't mean to …

PATTY
> Goodbye.

SIMON
Here, you can take the book if you want.

PATTY
I don't want it.

SIMON
Go on. Please.

PATTY
Why?

SIMON
Because I'm sorry, and I want you to. You keep asking me so many questions, maybe this will answer them for you.

PATTY takes the book.

PATTY
I don't think I'm the one with the questions, Simon.

PATTY leaves the treehouse. SIMON watches her go, then returns to his normal position.

SIMON
I don't feel too well.

A tired and exhausted SIMON lies down on the floor. A moment passes before an older Native man, CLYDE, approaches the tree. He looks up at the sleeping SIMON.

CLYDE
Hey, boy, you awake?

SIMON
    Go away.

CLYDE
    Have some respect there. Just because you're
    looking down on me doesn't mean you can
    look down on me. (*laughing*) That's a good
    one, huh?

    No response.

CLYDE
    I guess you don't remember me, eh?

    SIMON peeks out of the treehouse.

SIMON
    Are you my vision? Please say you are.

CLYDE
    Sorry. I'm no vision. Except one of beauty. Get
    it, a vision of beauty. (*laughs again*) You're not
    laughing, boy.

SIMON
    You're Native.

CLYDE
    Yeah, it helps when you're born on a Reserve.
    I'm your Uncle Clyde, Simon. Gosh, you look
    like your mother. I can't count the number of
    times I had to chase that mother of yours down
    from trees. She was like a little monkey, that
    one. I can see you take after her. Never had a
    treehouse, though, but sure did have a

fondness for wild apples. I remember this
time …

SIMON
Uncle Clyde?! What are you doing here?

CLYDE
Getting a crick in my neck looking up at you. I
was in town at a conference when I got a call
from home. Your father's been burning up the
telephone lines back home. Figured I'd come
and have a word with you. What are you doing
up there, boy?

SIMON
Trying to have a vision quest.

CLYDE
A vision quest?! (*quiet for a moment*) Well, that's
kind of stupid. If your mother knew you were
doing something foolish like that she'd—

SIMON
But aren't Native people supposed to do stuff
like this?

SIMON passes a book to CLYDE.

CLYDE
What is this? You want to be a bookstore
Indian? You can't learn how to do a vision quest
from a book. It's not something you do on a
weekend, like a camping trip or a slumber
party. What you're doing is sitting up in a tree
starving yourself. All this is going to accomplish

is to make you sick and maybe have a few hallucinations or something. Simon, a vision quest takes training and preparation. If you're serious about learning this stuff, you come out and visit us. The Elders will teach you. What possessed you to do something like this?

SIMON

I think I'm losing Mom, Uncle Clyde. I want to get her back. This way, I can maybe find her again, and maybe this is my way of, I don't know, honouring her anniversary.

CLYDE

You don't honour sombody's death, you honour their life. You won't find your mother up in that tree, only caterpillars.

SIMON is silent.

CLYDE

Simon ...

No response.

CLYDE

Okay, I'm going to have a word with your father for a while. But I better warn you, Simon, I have a chainsaw in the back of my truck.

CLYDE makes a buzzing sound as he exits. Still silent, SIMON waits. Before long, the sound of PATTY approaching can be heard through the trees.

SIMON
I've been waiting for you. I have to ask you something.

PATTY
Sounds serious. Here's your book, by the way.

SIMON
Thanks. Anyways, this is going to sound weird, but I got to ask it. Are you real?

PATTY
Wow. I've never been asked that. I think so, why?

SIMON
I was told you might be a hallucination or something. I just want to make sure.

PATTY
Me? Like maybe part of your vision or something? That is so cool. I've never been a vision before.

SIMON
This is serious. It's important. I want to know what's going on.

SIMON pinches PATTY, who cries out. PATTY responds by punching SIMON in the shoulder.

PATTY
Ouch. Tell you what, Simon. The last time I checked, which was this morning, I was pretty sure I was real. Woke up in my pyjamas, had a shower, ate waffles for breakfast, brushed my

teeth. I don't think visions do things like that. Then again, maybe I woke up in my imaginary pajamas, showered with make-believe water, ate non-existent waffles and brushed my fake teeth to prevent pretend cavities. Now there's a full day. Or was it actually a real day?

SIMON

This is not funny.

PATTY

I read your book.

SIMON

The whole thing?

PATTY

Yeah, I found it kind of interesting. But you're doing everything wrong. This whole vision quest thing is supposed to be looking forward, not behind.

SIMON

What's that supposed to mean?

PATTY

Not only are you doing the whole thing wrong—you know, no Elder supervision or training and all that—but the reason you're doing this is wrong.

SIMON

I don't need you to tell me what I'm doing. I'm the Native person, remember?

PATTY
Well, I think you're doing this vision quest thing like a White person would do it. It says so in the book. Look here ...

PATTY picks up the book and opens it.

SIMON
You take that back.

PATTY
Why? It's the truth. See!

SIMON
I thought you told me not to believe in all these books.

PATTY
That was yesterday. Simon, do you know what your problem is? Your treehouse, your vision quest, your mother. It's you, you, you. This Native ritual is not just yours, your mother is not just yours, everything you've been talking about has been about just you. It's not just you. Your father lost your mother, too! It's everything and everybody. Wow, that sounds deep.

SIMON sits down hard on the floor of the treehouse. He does not look well.

PATTY
What's wrong?

SIMON

I don't know. I just don't feel right. Maybe you're right. Maybe I should give this up. Maybe I'm not Native enough.

PATTY

There you go again. It has nothing to do with how Native you are. You should read those books more closely, or find somebody who knows what they're talking about. It says that White people have even been known to go on these vision quests. And contrary to what you think, even girls have been allowed. See, you don't know everything. (*pause*) Do you need any help? Should I go get your father?

SIMON

I miss my mother.

PATTY enters the treehouse again.

PATTY

What was she like?

SIMON

My mom. She'd make French toast with real cinnamon bread. Boy, I'd like some right now. My dad tries to make it, but he just can't get it right. I remember her being tall, but that was a long time ago. She probably wasn't much taller than you are. Glasses like yours. Dad says she was small. She had long, dark hair, brown eyes and real white teeth. I remember that, 'cause she used to smile a lot.

PATTY
  She sounds nice.

SIMON
  And when it was time for me to go to bed, she
  used to sing me a song, to make me fall asleep.
  I think it was a Native song. It had that feel to
  it. I think.

PATTY
  What did it sound like?

SIMON
  I don't … I can't …

PATTY
  Did it have words or did she just hum it?

SIMON
  I think she just hummed it.

PATTY
  Did it go something like this?

  PATTY hums a little tune.

SIMON
  No. Nothing like that.

PATTY
  Wish I could help more. But I just don't know
  many Native songs.

  *SIMON seems to be thinking. Something's coming
  to him. But he's struggling for it. He hums a few
  bars, starting over once or twice. He is fighting to*

> *catch the rhythm. He manages to hum a few bars*
> *when PATTY joins in and finishes it. SIMON is*
> *stunned that PATTY knows it.*

SIMON

How do you know that song?

PATTY

It's "Amazing Grace," you idiot! Everybody
knows that song. It's a hymn. It's not Indian.

SIMON

It's not? But my mother …

PATTY

Probably learned it in church or something.

> *PATTY starts humming the song again, and*
> *SIMON soon joins in. PATTY begins to sing the*
> *words. SIMON watches her closely, drawn in.*
> *SIMON begins to tremble. He is crying. SIMON*
> *falls over crying and PATTY goes to comfort him.*
> *It takes a moment, but soon SIMON begins to*
> *calm down.*

SIMON

You sound just like her. So much like her.

PATTY

You really should eat something. It's making
you a little nuts.

SIMON

(*embarrassed*) I'm sorry. I didn't mean that to
happen.

PATTY
    Are you okay now?

SIMON
    Yeah, I'm cool. It's just that I was thinking about my mother and … and … it just sort of happened.

PATTY
    I won't tell anyone if you won't.

SIMON
    You got a deal.

    THE FATHER walks out of the house and approaches the treehouse.

FATHER
    Simon, I've been talking with Clyde about your going to the Reserve, and I think it's a good idea. They'll teach you everything you need to know, and take care of you. And it will be a lot safer. It's better than you doing this alone.

SIMON
    Just a moment, Dad.

    SIMON retreats back into the treehouse.

SIMON
    (*to PATTY*) What do you think?

PATTY
    I've been telling you all along what I think. Are you having fun right now?

SIMON
No.

PATTY
Do you feel fine?

SIMON
No.

PATTY
Seriously, do you know what you're doing?

Pause.

SIMON
No.

PATTY
And more importantly, if something really goes wrong, do you know what to do? (*SIMON is silent.*) Besides, I think what you're looking for is down there, not up here.

SIMON peeks out of the treehouse toward his FATHER.

SIMON
Dad, I'll be down in a second.

FATHER
I'll be waiting, son.

SIMON returns to PATTY.

SIMON
Want to come down and meet my father?

PATTY
Uh, maybe later.

SIMON
Okay. And, Patty, thanks a lot.

PATTY
I'll save you some of my mom's apple pie.

SIMON
Food. That would be so great.

> *SIMON lowers the ladder to the ground and steps onto the top rung.*

SIMON
I'll see you later?

PATTY
I'll always be here.

SIMON
Bye.

PATTY
Bye.

> *SIMON begins climbing down. His FATHER is at the bottom to help him down. His FATHER hugs him close, then begins leading the weak SIMON back to the house.*

FATHER
Now, let's get some food into you. How about some apple waffles? They were your mother's favourite.

SIMON
  Dad, what was Mom's middle name?

FATHER
  Patricia. Why?

SIMON
  That's what I thought.

  They disappear into the house. Lights go down.

  The End.

GIRL WHO LOVED HER HORSES

Girl Who Loved Her Horses was produced by Theatre Direct Canada and premiered at the Theatre Centre in Toronto in April 1995 with the following cast:

DANIELLE: Michelle Thrush
RALPH: Warren Arcan
WILLIAM: Herbie Barnes
SHELLEY: Carol Greyeyes
THE HORSE: Levi Aguonie

Directed by Richard Greenblatt
Set design by Julie Fox
Costume design by Stephanie Tjelios
Lighting design by Jim Plaxton
Original music by Marsha Coffey
Movement by Denise Fujiwara

Cast
Danielle: A small, shy, timid ten-year-old girl
Ralph: A sensitive eleven-year-old boy
William: A rough, artistic eleven-year-old boy
Shelley: An older, practical sister of Ralph's
The Horse: The personification of Danielle's dream

Although the play begins and ends with the main characters in adulthood, it primarily depicts them remembering themselves as children.

Setting
The play begins and ends in a rundown part of the city, a gritty urban environment. The middle section of the play takes place on a Native reservation approximately three hours from the city (here it is Toronto, but it could be any city).

Time
Now. And then.

Production Notes
Girl Who Loved Her Horses is a difficult play to stage. I remember thinking when I wrote it, "I have no idea how they are going to do this, but that's what they get paid the big bucks for."

First, the play's timeline shifts back and forth between the past and the present, between the childhood and adult lives of the characters.

Second, it incorporates elements of dance. I imagine that the horse is dancing anytime Danielle draws it out of the wall; this is how Theatre Direct Canada staged the play. Dance is the horse's mode of expression, and, if done well, brings a truly beautiful element to the story.

Third, numerous settings are required, including multiple interior and exterior environments. The set design must necessarily be very versatile.

The play does not have a definitive ending. I have left it up to the audience to decide what happened to poor Danielle. One day, I hope to find this out for myself.

Scene One

*The lights come up on a cold and stark rundown
city street. Along one side of the set is an aged
and worn brick wall, covered in bills and posters.
A young Native man, RALPH, makes his way
across the street in no particular hurry.*

*His attention is caught by the posters advertising
a Native rally or festival, and he goes over to
investigate. He reads them as he walks along the
wall when something from above grabs his eye,
perhaps a flash of light or colour.*

*Backing up and looking above the posters, he
freezes in recognition, awed and overcome. There,
peeking above the posters, is the outline of what
appears to be an old and faded mural. The only
easily identifiable elements in the mural are the
terrifying and angry animalistic eyes, barely
above the paper posters, staring down at the silent
RALPH. There is also the hint of a mane
framing what might be the head. The colours and
savagery of the mural trigger something in the
stunned RALPH.*

*He approaches the wall again and rips away a
few handfuls of poster and bills to reveal more of
THE HORSE. The mural is drawn with chalk,
and half of it has been washed away by rain,
leaving it blurry in places, giving the impression*

*that part of the animal has been melted by heat.
It is an old beat-up image on an equally beat-up
wall, but there is still power.*

RALPH
Ho-lee!

*The lights go down on RALPH and up on THE
HORSE at another part of the stage. THE
HORSE, alone onstage, executes, through dance
and movement, an expression of its raging anger.
Both it and the dance should be terrifying and
bold.*

Scene Two

A typical Reserve household, three hours from the city. It is early evening and the room is dark. At the table sits a depressed SHELLEY. She remains unmoving in the shadows, barely breathing. Then footsteps are heard and somebody whistling. A door is thrown open with gusto and WILLIAM enters the room, covered in grease, dirt and paint.

WILLIAM

I'm gonna kill that American. I just need one more thing to push me over the edge. That's all. Do you know what he wants now? He wants sharks on that damn boat. Sharks! What the hell do I know about painting sharks! I tried to explain to the guy that muskies make better sense. The lake's full of them and that's what he wants to go out and catch. Gave him the old Indian line about honouring the spirit of the fish he's about to hunt. Didn't buy it. Sharks or nothing on the hull of that boat, he said. I can paint a lot of things but only stuff that makes sense, you know. Sharks in these freshwater lakes, I mean, think about it, buddy. Actually he heard me saying that to myself and, well, it looks like he's not going to buy the twenty-footer. There goes $30,000. So how was your day?

SHELLEY
  I quit.

WILLIAM
  Quit what?

SHELLEY
  Work. I quit work.

WILLIAM
  What do you mean you quit work?! You can't
  quit work!

SHELLEY
  I've just had it. I can't take the daycare another
  day. The kids yelling, the staff, everything. I
  have reached a point of no return. And that
  means I am definitely not returning.

WILLIAM
  But, Shelley ...

SHELLEY
  That kid was the last straw. I couldn't take
  anymore.

WILLIAM
  What kid?

SHELLEY
  That Benojee kid. You know, the one I've been
  telling you about. The one that draws all these
  black pictures. Not even pictures, just covers the
  paper in a coating of black crayon. One right
  after the other. Weirdest thing I ever saw.

WILLIAM
You quit over that?

SHELLEY
He bit me today when I tried to get him to draw
with a different colour. Bit me! Right there! All
because I put a red crayon in his hand. That
was it. I said to myself, "I don't need this
anymore." So I quit.

WILLIAM
We need the money.

SHELLEY
Sell the marina.

WILLIAM
Not my marina. I love this marina.

SHELLEY
Then learn to run it properly. Your American
was practically drooling over that boat. That
$30,000 could get us through the winter, and I
happen to be quite fond of being warm.

WILLIAM
So am I but, sweetie, I can't draw a shark. Tried
and tried. Ended up looking like a pickerel with
an attitude. It just wasn't meant to be. Sorry, no
sale.

SHELLEY
You no sale, me no job, we no eat.

WILLIAM
Maybe you'll reconsider and go back to work
tomorrow?

SHELLEY
Don't think so. Maybe you'll reconsider the
shark?

WILLIAM
Don't think so.

SHELLEY
Welfare's sounding better and better.

WILLIAM
I can't go on Welfare. I used to be the Chief of
this Reserve. How will that look?

SHELLEY
Don't give me that. You didn't care how things
looked when you were Chief. You
misappropriated funds to build this damn
place. People are calling it William's Watergate
Marina.

WILLIAM
Hey, I'm gonna pay them back. In a few more
years when the marina …

SHELLEY
"In a few years, in a few years." You know how
many times I've heard that? Or "next spring
when the boats are in the water we'll start
making real money." It's going to take more
than a few years. I do the books, remember.

Nobody comes here from the village. They don't trust you.

WILLIAM begins to hunt through the cupboards.

WILLIAM
I think you're being a little selfish.

SHELLEY
Selfish! I'm being selfish. You won't paint a stupid shark on a $30,000 boat to keep us warm this winter and I'm selfish! (*pause*) William, I'm tired of being underpaid, understaffed and overwhelmed. The council doesn't appreciate what I do there, some of the kids would just as soon take a chunk out of you as take a nap and ... oh, why am I talking to you anyways. It's like talking to a three-year-old.

WILLIAM
We got any cookies? I'm tellin' ya, Ralph should have gone into business with me like I asked him. Boy, we would have really had this place rockin' then. Me doin' the boats, you the books, he could handle all the people. Folks like him. He'd have customers eatin' out of his hands. He'd have convinced that American to keep the fish on the boat.

SHELLEY
Don't drag him into your fantasy world. He's happy studying to be a cop. You know him, he always wanted to be a good guy.

WILLIAM
So what are we going to do about your job?

SHELLEY
I don't know. Maybe get another one.

WILLIAM
Your diploma says Early Childhood Education,
it's either that or a McDonald's. And the
Reserve doesn't have a McDonald's.

SHELLEY
I am not going back to that place!

The door opens and RALPH enters.

RALPH
What place?

SHELLEY
Ralph?! What are you doing here?

*RALPH drops his duffle bag on the floor, not
answering. Instead, he approaches the far white
wall.*

SHELLEY
Is something wrong? Are you okay?

RALPH
Yeah, I'm fine.

RALPH stops and gazes at the wall.

WILLIAM
That's a wall, Ralph.

RALPH
I know. I just wanted to come home. See the
place.

SHELLEY
It's not like you to come home mid-week.

RALPH
It happens.

WILLIAM
Hey, Ralph, do you think sharks belong on the
side of those boats out there?

RALPH
What?

SHELLEY
Stop trying to get him on your side.

WILLIAM
He's in college; he knows these things.

SHELLEY
I don't believe you're giving me a hard time on
this. It's just paint on fibreglass. Last month,
somebody wanted a deer on a canoe. You didn't
put up a fight then.

WILLIAM
The woods are full of deer. I've seen deer.
You've seen deer. Even that American has seen
deer. They belong here. But there's no point in
drawing a shark. I don't know anything about
sharks. I've never seen a shark. There are no

sharks in these waters, so there's no sharks on
the boat.

RALPH
The Inuit.

SHELLEY
What?

RALPH
They're famous for their carvings.

SHELLEY
What are you talking about? Do you know?

WILLIAM
Don't look at me, he's *your* brother.

RALPH
To the traditionally minded Inuit, the purpose
of carving was to let free the image or spirit
trapped within the stone. Once the image was
free, and the stone carved, they would move on.
They were a nomadic people; the concept of
carrying around big stone carvings just wasn't
practical.

SHELLEY
Well, there's nothing more practical than eating
and keeping warm.

RALPH
Like the wall.

WILLIAM

What wall? Pink Floyd's *The Wall*? The big one they have in China?

RALPH

We covered it over in layers and layers of paint like we were trying to hide it or get rid of it. It's still there, like the hundreds and hundreds of Inuit carvings scattered all through the Arctic, almost forgotten, hidden behind that wall.

WILLIAM

What's hidden?

SHELLEY

Uh, Ralph, are you okay?

RALPH

I'd almost forgotten all the things I'd seen on this wall, all the images, pictures, stories we had put on it. We used to kneel right there, by the refrigerator. Remember that?

SHELLEY

Ralph, are you talking about the Everything Wall?

RALPH

Right there, that's where the head would be, and over there was where the mane would extend to. That whole wall would be taken up, just flaming with colour. Remember how we used to just stand there and stare at it for hours? It gave me goosebumps.

WILLIAM
He's talking about that horse. The one that
little girl drew.

SHELLEY
Danielle.

RALPH
That's her name. Danielle. I haven't thought
about her in years. Not until I saw that horse
again. I saw it today. It was hard to tell it was a
horse, let alone the same one. You couldn't
look at those eyes and not remember it over
there, on that wall. Except this time, it was
different. It was as big as this house, drawn
across a rundown brick building in a dirty part
of town. It was something about the eyes. They
used to be so, so wild and free, you remember
them. But this time they were colder, darker. I
wanted to see them the way they used to be,
back when we were kids. That's why I came
home.

SHELLEY
You came home to the Everything Wall?

RALPH
How old were we then? Ten, twelve ...?

SHELLEY
Yeah, something like that. I think you were in
Grade Five. Wasn't that the year William failed?

WILLIAM
I didn't fail, I was left behind.

RALPH
Yeah, that was around the time of the
Everything Wall.

Scene Three

The sound of crunching pervades the stage, little mouse-like chewing sounds as DANIELLE walks across a playground eating from a bag of chips. She meticulously eats one after the other as she walks. She walks slowly, as if she has no place to go. She holds her school books across her body. She looks nervous for no apparent reason.

Then from offstage, the sound of shouting and running can be heard. Two young boys rush onstage, one after the other.

RALPH
  You run about as good as you smell. Awful.

WILLIAM
  Let's see how good you smell when I break your nose.

  WILLIAM lunges after RALPH and tackles him. They go down in a pile of arms and legs. WILLIAM jumps up with a triumphant yell.

WILLIAM
  You're it!

  RALPH races after him and is almost touching him when WILLIAM aims for DANIELLE and swerves at the last moment before RALPH has a chance to react. RALPH runs bang into

*DANIELLE, sending her, her books and her
potato chips flying.*

RALPH

Oh, sorry, um here.

*RALPH is embarrassed and a little concerned.
He makes a token effort to pick up some of her
books. RALPH quickly hands them, almost
tossing them, to the fallen DANIELLE.*

WILLIAM

You're still it, and you'll always be it.

*WILLIAM darts away quickly as Ralph makes a
lunge for him. DANIELLE is forgotten in the
mayhem. The boys disappear offstage, running at
full gallop, leaving DANIELLE alone onstage,
books and chips askew.*

DANIELLE

That's okay.

*DANIELLE looks at the mess of spilled potato
chips surrounding her. There is one left in the
bag and she delicately eats it. Then she gets on
her knees and picks up all the remaining chips
on the ground and places them neatly in the bag,
and then in a nearby garbage can. She gathers
the rest of her stuff and walks to a nearby swing,
where she sits down and tries to put her books
together.*

*There is silence for a moment, then from the
opposite end of the stage the sound of boyish yells*

get gradually louder and closer until the two boys come racing out again, running flat out. This time RALPH is in the lead with WILLIAM behind him. RALPH then sees SHELLEY entering the playground. RALPH immediately stops, does a 180 to avoid her and runs directly into WILLIAM, their heads knocking together with a loud thud. They both, once again, go down in a heap. This time, however, they don't get up as fast, and moan in pain. SHELLEY approaches them as they lie rolling on the ground. Behind them, DANIELLE is swinging ever so slightly on the swing.

RALPH
Oh, my head … I think I can feel my brain.

WILLIAM
Somebody look up my nose and tell me if it's bleeding.

SHELLEY
Oh, gross. Get away from me. Ralph, Mom wants to know how many people are coming over tonight.

WILLIAM
Coming over for what?

SHELLEY ignores him.

SHELLEY
I've invited Julia, Vanessa and Anita.

WILLIAM
   To what?

RALPH
   I didn't invite anybody.

SHELLEY
   Why not?

RALPH
   I didn't want to.

WILLIAM
   Want to what? What am I missing here?

SHELLEY
   You know Mom's looking forward to it. She's
   promised a prize and everything to the best
   one.

WILLIAM
   Prize?! There's a prize?! What do I have to do?

RALPH
   Shelley, it might turn into something stupid like
   that time Mom bought that cow.

WILLIAM
   (*laughing*) I remember that. Your mom is so
   funny! She wanted to cut down on all the
   money she spent on milk and butter and
   cheese. So she bought all that cow stuff. And it
   wasn't even a milk cow.

SHELLEY
> It wasn't even a female cow. Mom didn't even check.

RALPH
> And then it ate everything in the vegetable garden.

WILLIAM
> And it left behind those huge piles of green smelly cow sh—

SHELLEY
> It was so embarrassing. I stayed at Grandma's for two weeks till things died down.

RALPH
> Oh, Mom's okay. She makes life interesting.

WILLIAM
> I'll say.

SHELLEY
> So you better invite some people over, for Mom's sake.

WILLIAM
> Invite them to what?

RALPH
> Mom wants us to draw things on our kitchen wall. She's calling it the Everything Wall because we're supposed to put everything we can think of on it.

WILLIAM
 Everything?

SHELLEY
 You behave. This is my mother's wall and I
 don't want you embarrassing us anymore than
 you already do.

WILLIAM
 Hey, Ralph, I saw this great movie on television
 where this guy had this painting of himself that
 kept getting older and older while he stayed the
 same. Let's draw paintings of how Shelley will
 look when she's really old, with things falling off,
 drool coming down her chin, big wrinkles all
 over the place. You know, five years down the
 road.

SHELLEY
 You're so immature. That's probably why you
 failed.

WILLIAM
 I didn't fail. I was left behind.

SHELLEY
 Big difference.

RALPH
 Let's not do it, Shell. We'll tell Mom we forgot
 or something. Maybe she'll forget about it in a
 few days.

SHELLEY
We have to do it. She's made room on that whole wall for this. Even moved the refrigerator over. Now, my friends will be finished around eight; then you can have it. I guess you'll have to bring him to draw with.

WILLIAM
Sure, I'll go. What's for dinner?

SHELLEY
Liver.

WILLIAM
I'll come later.

SHELLEY
Mom's counting on us, Ralph.

SHELLEY turns to leave. RALPH and WILLIAM start walking in a different direction.

RALPH
Why does Mom do these things?

WILLIAM
Are you really having liver?

DANIELLE stops swinging.

DANIELLE
The Everything Wall.

Scene Four

DANIELLE leaves the swings and journeys home in her typical meek manner. She arrives at her front door and stops, nervous. Loud, angry noises can be heard. DANIELLE appears afraid to enter. She finally musters up the nerve and enters the house, making a beeline for her room, where she immediately crawls into bed, letting the books that are on top fall to the ground. The noises grow louder, and DANIELLE crawls under the covers, seeking protection.

DANIELLE wraps the blankets around her tiny body and crawls into a corner, racked with shivers. The noise of a violent argument can be heard on the other side of the wall. Each loud bellow makes DANIELLE shiver in fear. As the yelling gets louder, she pulls the blanket higher and higher until she disappears beneath the covers. The covers hiding her tremble occasionally.

Then a blurred, or not-quite-realized, image of THE HORSE appears on the wall, or more accurately, behind the wall. He moves along the length of the wall, behind DANIELLE, as if seeking an opening. He tries to reach out to the little girl but the wall prevents him from making contact.

Scene Five

SHELLEY is sitting at the kitchen table, playing solitaire. WILLIAM and RALPH enter and immediately grab pop from the refrigerator. The Everything Wall is partially covered in designs of various things and levels of talent.

WILLIAM
Hey, Shelley, where are your friends? Didn't show, huh?

SHELLEY
Oh, they were here, and, Ralph, you should have heard the things they were telling me about William.

WILLIAM
What? What did they say?

SHELLEY
Wouldn't you like to know?

WILLIAM
Well ... yeah ...

RALPH
You actually drew on this thing, huh?

SHELLEY
>(*pointing*) That's mine. Wait till you see what I
>have in mind for next week. It's so great.
>Wanna know?

RALPH
>Nah.

>>*WILLIAM surveys the range of art and starts to
>>laugh.*

WILLIAM
>You call this art?! Come on, I've seen better
>drawings in kindergarten. What's this supposed
>to be?

SHELLEY
>None of your business.

WILLIAM
>Tell me.

SHELLEY
>It's that cow we used to own. Happy?

WILLIAM
>This is yours! How'd you remember what it
>looked like? Use a mirror?

RALPH
>What is it with you? She's *my* sister, not yours. I
>should be the one always fighting with her.

WILLIAM
Nah, it's always open season on your sister. I'm just lucky enough to get in the first shots. What do you call it, a turkey shoot?

SHELLEY makes a jump for WILLIAM, wanting to punch him. RALPH holds her back.

SHELLEY
Just one shot, Ralph, that's all I want. That's all I need.

RALPH
Mom!

SHELLEY
Forget it, she's not here. She's driving my friends home.

SHELLEY goes back to her cards while WILLIAM surveys the wall.

WILLIAM
My mother would have put me up for adoption if she saw me drawing stuff like that on our kitchen wall.

RALPH
Well, have fun. We're going down to the lake.

SHELLEY
You're not going to draw anything?

RALPH
I can't be bothered.

SHELLEY
You'd better draw something. Maybe it will help
you in art class.

*Grabbing a pencil crayon, RALPH approaches
the wall. He draws a foot-long vertical line,
studies it for a moment, then draws another one
parallel to it. He quickly adds two horizontal
lines, thereby making a tic-tac-toe.*

RALPH
Wanna play?

WILLIAM
Only if I can win.

*They begin to play games while SHELLEY
continues with her card game. WILLIAM cheats
by putting an extra X on the wall when RALPH
isn't looking.*

WILLIAM
So, Shelley, what did Vanessa and Julia say
about me?

SHELLEY
Nothing much. It was what Anita said that was
interesting.

*WILLIAM gets all embarrassed and turns away
from SHELLEY and RALPH.*

RALPH
Just go.

WILLIAM starts a new game.

WILLIAM
How come you're doing so bad in art? It's easy.

RALPH
It's boring. That and the fact I can't draw might have something to do with it.

WILLIAM
Everybody can draw. You just put lines on paper.

SHELLEY finishes her card game and walks over to take a look at what the boys are doing.

SHELLEY
Not exactly great art, boys. Unlike these masterpieces. And William, Anita drew that one.

WILLIAM
So what? Looks like a strangled chicken.

SHELLEY
It's a dog.

WILLIAM
You can prove this?

RALPH
You're doing it again.

WILLIAM
Ralph, the rain falls, dogs bark, we fight. Get used to it.

RALPH
Well, I'll say one thing. I think Shelley's going
to win the prize.

SHELLEY
Get used to it.

> *As though a challenge has been thrown down,
> WILLIAM grabs a pencil and draws, with a few
> quick strokes, a startlingly realistic image of a
> teepee.*

WILLIAM
Now, what was this you were saying about a
prize?

SHELLEY
Big deal.

> *There is a quiet knock, so quiet nobody hears it
> except RALPH. He cocks his head.*

WILLIAM
Jealous?

SHELLEY
In your dreams.

WILLIAM
Wanna try your hand at some real cards?

SHELLEY
No.

WILLIAM
Afraid I'll beat you at that, too?

SHELLEY
Oh, drop dead and die.

WILLIAM
Aren't those two the same thing? Hey, Ralph,
wanna play some cards?

RALPH
Huh? Oh sure.

WILLIAM
Last chance there, Shell.

SHELLEY
Oh, very well, just to teach you a lesson.

WILLIAM
Crazy eights. My deal.

> *They sit down at the table. WILLIAM starts to
> deal. Then there is a very quiet, barely audible
> scratching/knocking. RALPH is the only one who
> hears it.*

RALPH
Hey, did you guys hear something?

WILLIAM
Like what?

RALPH
I don't know. It was just something out of the
corner of my ear.

WILLIAM
(*laughing*) Corner of your ear? Good one,
Ralph. So what do you think my prize is gonna
be?

SHELLEY
You're so sure it's you, aren't you? There's some
other good stuff up there, too. You're not the
only one who can draw.

WILLIAM
I hope it's money.

> *The same noise repeats, this time just a little bit
> louder.*

SHELLEY
I heard it that time.

RALPH
The door maybe?

WILLIAM
Awful wimpy knock if it is.

> *SHELLEY goes to investigate. When she pulls the
> door open, DANIELLE is standing there, looking
> smaller than ever.*

SHELLEY
Who are you?

> *DANIELLE, the poster girl for shyness, doesn't
> respond. The other kids look, surprised to see her.*

WILLIAM
(*secretly to RALPH*) Oh, man, Ralph, look who it is. The dumb girl.

RALPH
She's not dumb.

WILLIAM
Sure acts like it sometimes.

SHELLEY
Aren't you gonna say something?

RALPH
She doesn't talk much. Doesn't do much of anything.

> *DANIELLE just stands there, looking more and more like the proverbial shrinking violet.*

SHELLEY
Well, you coming in?

> *DANIELLE hesitates for a moment.*

SHELLEY
What are you afraid of? I said "come in."

> *DANIELLE manages to enter the kitchen.*

RALPH
Hey, Danielle.

SHELLEY
Danielle, that's a pretty name. I was thinking of changing my name to Kateri when I get older,

you know, after the Indian saint. Better than
Shelley. So what do you want, kid?

*DANIELLE mumbles something, but it's
impossible to make it out.*

SHELLEY
Tell me, I won't bite.

WILLIAM
Don't believe it.

DANIELLE struggles to speak louder.

DANIELLE
I heard you could draw here.

SHELLEY
Yeah, do you wanna?

DANIELLE shyly nods her head.

SHELLEY
Well, okay, the pencil crayons are over there.
There's still a lot of room left, big space over
there. (*pointing*) That's my house there; don't
you just love the tulips? I saw this house once
when we went to the city. That's where I want to
live when I get out of school. So draw what you
want, my mom gives a prize every Monday night
to the best picture. She won't tell us what the
prize is, though. And then she washes it off for
Tuesday. Okay?

DANIELLE
Thank you.

DANIELLE shyly approaches the Everything Wall. She walks around the card players and tries to reach the pencil crayons, but they are too high for her. She jumps up but still can't reach them.

WILLIAM
Will you hurry up, Shelley? It's your turn.

SHELLEY grabs the pencils and hands them to DANIELLE.

SHELLEY
Here. (*to RALPH*) Did you watch him? He didn't cheat did he?

DANIELLE
(*in an unnoticed voice*) Thank you.

She examines her pencils closely, and removes five specific colours. The others she puts on the counter. She stands there and looks at the wall.

SHELLEY
Danielle? You live around here?

DANIELLE
My mom and I live across the tracks.

SHELLEY
Oh, so you aren't part of the Reserve?

DANIELLE
No.

SHELLEY
Who's your mom?

WILLIAM
Elsie Fiddler.

SHELLEY reacts to that. It does not look like good news. She speaks to RALPH in hushed tones.

SHELLEY
Ohh. You in her class?

RALPH
Yeah, but that's about it. We don't hang around with her or anything. I don't think I've ever seen her hang out with anybody.

SHELLEY
No friends? Do you guys pick on her or tease her?

WILLIAM
No, you've got to have a personality to be picked on.

SHELLEY
What?

WILLIAM
Something for people to make fun of. She doesn't have enough to tease.

RALPH
She's sort of like a shadow.

WILLIAM
Just a dull blob, not making any noise or drawing attention to herself.

SHELLEY
  Oh, how sad.

WILLIAM
  Yeah, I guess. Can we go back to the game now?

  *SHELLEY, WILLIAM and RALPH focus on the
  card game, completely unaware of DANIELLE
  and what she's about to go through. DANIELLE
  puts pencil crayon to wall and THE HORSE
  comes through the wall slowly. He is skittish
  around her, checking out his space. She moves
  toward him. He looks slightly dangerous, but
  she's not afraid.*

  *THE HORSE glows with energy, radiating
  everything that DANIELLE isn't. It has strength,
  confidence, freedom. Power. DANIELLE slowly,
  carefully continues to approach THE HORSE.
  She reaches out, her hands desperate to touch
  him, and at the same time afraid he'll disappear
  the moment they make contact. He swings her
  around, fast and amazing at first, then tenderly.
  She slides down the front of THE HORSE slowly,
  her back against him, her face glowing. She
  makes a huge sound of joy and release. She
  laughs and giggles like the child she has a right
  to be.*

DANIELLE
  I knew you'd be there. I knew it.

  *She closes her eyes, still radiant. THE HORSE
  slips away from her and back through the wall.
  She turns to find him gone. There is a moment of*

*sadness as she allows the power to leave her. She
goes toward the wall.*

*A large, magnificent creation of THE HORSE is
on the wall. DANIELLE puts the last touch on
her creation and then neatly puts the remaining
pencil crayons back into their package.*

SHELLEY
Ralph, I think he was cheating, but I don't
know how.

WILLIAM
(*cocky*) Too fast for you, huh?

DANIELLE
Thank you.

She exits.

RALPH
So you *were* cheating!

WILLIAM
I never said that. You can't prove it.

*Upset, SHELLEY throws the cards on the table
and storms away. She is the first to see THE
HORSE.*

SHELLEY
Uh, guys …

*The two boys follow SHELLEY's line of sight and
see THE HORSE. They get up to get a better view.*

They all stand there, eyes wide, amazed and silent for a few moments.

RALPH
Nice horse!

SHELLEY
Amazing!

WILLIAM
Ultra-amazing! That was Danielle, wasn't it?

They all approach the wall. RALPH reaches out and touches the wall to make sure it's real.

SHELLEY
That shy little girl ...

WILLIAM
It's almost like it's alive. Where'd she learn that?!

RALPH
Not with our art teacher. I think it's looking at me.

SHELLEY
This can't be washed off. It would be a sin, like painting over the Sixteen Chapel.

RALPH
That's *Sistine* Chapel.

SHELLEY
A sin's a sin, Ralph, no matter what you call it. I think I want to look at this every day.

WILLIAM
Gotta admit, it is beautiful.

SHELLEY
We should put a frame around it.

WILLIAM
Maybe charge admission.

SHELLEY
I'll ask Mom if we can keep it.

> *The three stand there and look at it for a
> ridiculously long time.*

RALPH
Nice horse.

WILLIAM
I'm not gonna win, am I?

> *In unison, RALPH and SHELLEY shake their
> heads, their eyes never leaving THE HORSE.*

Scene Six

The next day, DANIELLE is walking across the schoolyard. RALPH and SHELLEY approach her and block her way. Instantly, she goes back into shrinking-violet mode.

SHELLEY
Hey, Danielle, that was some horse you drew.

RALPH
Yep, never seen one like it before.

DANIELLE
Thank you.

SHELLEY
Um, my mom says you're welcome over at our place anytime you want.

DANIELLE
Thank you.

> *There is an uncomfortable silence. RALPH nudges SHELLEY.*

SHELLEY
Oh, and this is for you.

> *SHELLEY takes something out of her knapsack and hands it to DANIELLE, who timidly takes it.*

*It is the prize, a book of pretty but cheap
paintings.*

DANIELLE
Thank you.

SHELLEY
Do you, like, ever say anything other than
"thank you"?

DANIELLE is thumbing through the book.

DANIELLE
Pretty pictures. Look, a horse.

*She continues to leaf through the book, oblivious
to SHELLEY and RALPH.*

SHELLEY
Well …

No reaction from DANIELLE.

RALPH
I guess we should be going now.

No reaction.

SHELLEY
Okay … ?! Bye.

RALPH
Bye, Danielle.

*They turn to leave. DANIELLE doesn't
acknowledge them.*

SHELLEY
    That is one strange puppy.

    They exit.

    After a few seconds, DANIELLE closes the book, a smile on her face. She continues her journey across the playground, the book held tightly in her hands. Lights come up on WILLIAM, straddling a swing and eating an apple. DANIELLE crosses in front of him. WILLIAM watches her for a moment, bored.

WILLIAM
    Hey, Danielle ...

    DANIELLE freezes instantly, not looking up, her lowered face hidden by her hair. She stays frozen in place as WILLIAM watches. Slightly amused, WILLIAM finishes his apple and tosses it at her feet, in disdain at her strangeness. He dismounts the swing as if it were a horse and walks away from her. DANIELLE does not move until WILLIAM has disappeared; then she picks up the apple core, walks a few feet and deposits it in a trash can.

Scene Seven

Later that week. The Everything Wall is covered with horses of every shape, description, colour and level of talent. RALPH is quietly doing his homework on the kitchen table. SHELLEY is doing her homework at the counter while talking on the phone.

SHELLEY

Yeah, you should see it, Julia. It's really amazing. There are horses everywhere. Everybody's drawing horses now. Pretty soon we'll need a corral.

Occasionally, RALPH gives SHELLEY an annoyed look.

SHELLEY

No, Danielle hasn't been here all week. (*pause*) Who knows. But I think it's between William and Vanessa's cousin for best horse, next to Danielle's, of course, but she can't win twice for the same picture. They both look really good but don't tell William I said that.

There is a quiet knock on the door.

SHELLEY

Julia, somebody's at the door. I'll call you right back.

*She hangs up the phone to open the door,
revealing DANIELLE.*

SHELLEY
Hey, come in. Do you want a pop or anything?

DANIELLE shakes her head as she enters.

SHELLEY
Boy, you really started something with that
horse of yours; take a look.

*DANIELLE sees the wall of horses but has eyes
only for hers.*

DANIELLE
It's still here.

SHELLEY
I know.

DANIELLE
But you said you get rid of them so we could do
new ones. That's what you're supposed to do.
It's still here.

SHELLEY
But it's so cool, we …

DANIELLE
I'm sorry. Thank you.

*DANIELLE turns and leaves immediately,
leaving behind a surprised household.*

SHELLEY
Danielle?! Wait. What's wrong?

DANIELLE is long gone. RALPH approaches the wall.

RALPH
Model airplanes.

SHELLEY
What?

RALPH
Model airplanes. Like, if someone gave me a model airplane, I wouldn't want to be given a finished one; I'd wanna put it together myself. After that, they get kind of boring. It's drawing the picture she likes, not the picture itself.

SHELLEY dials the phone.

SHELLEY
Well, I think it's stupid. Julia? Yeah, that was her. She is so weird. She looked like she was insulted or something, or didn't want to see the horse. There's still room for her to draw something else. Like, what's her problem? Anyways, I'll be right over. Don't do anything till I get there, okay? Bye.

SHELLEY hangs up and throws on her jacket.

SHELLEY
I'm going to Julia's. Tell Mom I'll be home for dinner.

She exits. RALPH, still looking at the wall, makes a mental decision. He locates a bucket of water, some soap and a sponge, then takes one last look at THE HORSE.

RALPH
Bye.

Scene Eight

SHELLEY, WILLIAM and RALPH are back in the kitchen, playing cards. SHELLEY is looking out the kitchen window at the miserable, rainy weather. WILLIAM is waiting for RALPH to deal.

SHELLEY
What a horrible day. I was going over to Vanessa's. I bet her and Julia are having fun.

WILLIAM
Who cares? Are we playing or what?

RALPH starts to deal the cards.

RALPH
Mom asked about Danielle again.

SHELLEY
Did you tell Danielle you washed it off?

RALPH
Course I did. She said "thank you" and then walked away.

WILLIAM
I think it has something to do with her mother, that Elsie Fiddler lady.

SHELLEY
   What does?

WILLIAM
   Her weirdo-ness. That's what my mom thinks. I
   heard her talkin' with my dad about all these
   parties she had and all her boyfriends. They say
   the police have even been over there a couple
   times.

RALPH
   What about her father?

WILLIAM
   They didn't say but I heard Elsie's new
   boyfriend just got out of jail.

SHELLEY
   You're kidding!

WILLIAM
   Nope, heard it myself. Beat up some woman
   over in Barrie.

SHELLEY
   Really? But, guys, we really shouldn't be talking
   about her behind her back.

WILLIAM
   Okay, let's do it in front of her.

   Nobody laughs.

WILLIAM
   It was a joke.

There is a quiet knock at the door. SHELLEY gets up and opens the door to reveal a wet, drowned-looking DANIELLE. She still has a spark in her eye.

SHELLEY
Hey, it's you.

SHELLEY ushers the dripping girl into the kitchen and takes her coat. SHELLEY grabs a dish towel and tries to dry DANIELLE's hair.

SHELLEY
You are a wet one, aren't you? You know where the pencil crayons are. Go to it.

DANIELLE approaches the wall but WILLIAM deliberately blocks her. She can't get around him and he pretends to be busy looking at his cards. He feels SHELLEY and RALPH staring at him in disgust and annoyance. He reluctantly moves out of her way.

DANIELLE picks up the pencil crayons. She removes five of them and studies a large blank section of the wall. RALPH watches her while SHELLEY and WILLIAM continue playing cards. DANIELLE selects her first pencil crayon and stares at the wall.

SHELLEY
Whose turn is it?

WILLIAM
 It's Ralph's. Hey, snap out of it. Are we playing
 or what?

RALPH
 I don't wanna play anymore.

> *RALPH leaves, obviously fascinated with*
> *DANIELLE and her drawing process. WILLIAM*
> *is frustrated at RALPH for leaving the game.*

WILLIAM
 What's with this stupid picture anyways? It's just
 some lines on the wall.

SHELLEY
 William, shh.

WILLIAM
 I just don't see what all the fuss is about.

SHELLEY
 You wouldn't.

WILLIAM
 Come on, Ralph, let's at least finish the game.

RALPH
 Play without me.

WILLIAM
 I'm sick of that horse. If she's such a great
 artist, let's see her do something else. Danielle,
 as a favour to me, please, draw me a ... a ...
 dog. Yeah, a dog.

SHELLEY
Maybe she doesn't want to.

WILLIAM
Sure she does. If she's an artist like everybody says, she should be able to draw anything. Oh, come on, there's more to life than just horses. I'm waiting for a dog!

DANIELLE shakes her head again.

DANIELLE
No. They bark.

SHELLEY
William, leave her alone.

WILLIAM
We were having a fun game of cards till she showed up. Did you know Ralph gave her a cute little nickname?

SHELLEY
Shut up, William, or I'm gonna …

WILLIAM
Girl Who Loved Her Horses. Should be Girl Who's Afraid to Draw a Stupid Dog. I wanna see a dog.

RALPH
William!

WILLIAM
I know my name. Danielle, draw a dog right there. (*He points.*)

DANIELLE turns hesitantly to the wall. There is a long pause as she tries to imagine the dog.

SHELLEY
Leave her alone.

WILLIAM
I'm not hurting her. I just want to see a dog. Horses are easy, dogs are harder.

Startled and nervous, she starts to draw but her movements lack the grace of her drawing of the horse. They are jerky, very unartistic. WILLIAM is watching her with fascination, then amusement. It is a very poor image of a dog.

WILLIAM
That's a dog. Boy, they must have some funny-looking dogs across the tracks. Looks like a cross between a chicken and a rhinoceros. Draw me something else. Draw me a … duck.

WILLIAM is laughing and DANIELLE is starting to cry softly.

SHELLEY
That's enough. You leave her alone this minute. Just get out.

WILLIAM
Fine, you want her for a friend, then have her. I got better things to do than this. I just wanted to show you she isn't all that hot. Come on, Ralph, let's get out of here.

RALPH
You go without me.

WILLIAM
(*surprised*) Ralph ...?

RALPH
Just go, William.

WILLIAM
Fine, I didn't want to stay here anyways.

> *Angry and embarrassed, WILLIAM storms to the
> door and flings it open to make a dramatic exit.
> As the door opens, there is a bright flash of
> lightning and a loud crack of thunder, making
> him pause at the door. Instead of turning around
> and losing face, he stubbornly gathers himself up
> and walks out into the pouring rain, slamming
> the door behind him.*

SHELLEY
What a goof.

RALPH
I wonder what made him do that?

SHELLEY
I don't know. He's your friend.

RALPH
Hey ...

> *They are so engrossed in their conversation that
> they barely hear the quiet crying of DANIELLE.
> Instantly concerned, SHELLEY and RALPH*

> *rush to her side. DANIELLE tries to crawl away
> and ends up in the corner.*

SHELLEY
  Hey, take it easy. He's gone.

RALPH
  Are you okay?

> *DANIELLE doesn't say anything; she just cries
> more.*

RALPH
  What should we do?

SHELLEY
  I don't know. What an idiot.

> *DANIELLE looks up.*

SHELLEY
  No, not you. William. You're okay.

DANIELLE
  He scares me.

SHELLEY
  He pisses me off. Come on, let's get you up off
  the floor.

> *They place her in a chair and SHELLEY wipes
> her eyes and nose.*

SHELLEY
  He's usually not as bad as that, but I think he's
  a little jealous of you.

DANIELLE
Me?

SHELLEY
Yep. Eh, Ralph?

RALPH
He's kinda used to being the centre of attention.

RALPH runs to the refrigerator and gets DANIELLE a pop. He pours it into a glass and hands it to DANIELLE.

DANIELLE
Thank you.

RALPH
Can I ask you a question?

DANIELLE shrugs nervously.

RALPH
Why do you draw that horse? I mean, that's an amazing horse.

DANIELLE shrugs again.

RALPH
Like, that's a bad dog. But your horse ...

DANIELLE
He's a beautiful horse, huh?

SHELLEY
Never saw one like it.

DANIELLE
That's my horse. Mine. He wasn't always there, but now he's there whenever I want him.

RALPH
Where'd it come from?

DANIELLE
Campbellford, I guess.

SHELLEY
Campbellford?! That town past Marmora?

DANIELLE
Uh-huh.

SHELLEY
Why there?

    DANIELLE shrugs again.

SHELLEY
You can tell us. Really.

DANIELLE
When I was six, back when my dad was alive, he took me to that fair they have in Campbellford. They had pony rides there. I remember this big lineup of kids, and there was only one pony for all those kids.

SHELLEY
Yeah, we had one of those at Indian Days, remember, Ralph?

DANIELLE

We had to stand in line for a long time before I got a chance to ride, and I kept watching that pony. They put one kid after another on his back and he would go around in a circle, and around and around, wearing out a path in the grass. Sometimes his eyes weren't even open. That's all he ever did. Just went around in a circle all day, every day. And I felt sad for him. He looked old, unhappy, and his back was bent. When it was my turn to ride, I started crying. I felt so sorry for that poor pony, I didn't want to ride him.

RALPH

What's that got to do with your horse?

DANIELLE

A couple months later my dad died. And things got different at home. And I never stopped thinking of that pony, thinking how sad its life must be. I wondered if he dreamed of better things when his eyes were closed. Then it began to change when I'd think of him; he grew bigger, got stronger, got real beautiful. And I began to wonder if all things could change, be different if they had better places to live, people who loved them. That makes me want to draw the horse even more. It makes the horse happy.

RALPH

Geez, your art teacher must really love you.

DANIELLE
    It doesn't work when it's on a small piece of
    paper. Then it becomes the pony again. It has
    to be someplace big, it has to be special. Your
    house is special. I tried it once on our wall.
    Mommy didn't like that. I got punished for
    that. That's why I wanted to come here.

RALPH
    Maybe we can come over to your place
    sometime.

    DANIELLE shakes her head vigorously.

DANIELLE
    No. Can't. Mommy's boyfriend is there. Don't
    like people coming to visit. (*She is quiet for a
    moment.*) I miss my dad. I miss my mommy.

RALPH
    But your mom's still alive.

DANIELLE
    It's not my same mommy. She's changed. She
    used to be so nice. Now I'm afraid.

SHELLEY
    Afraid of what?

DANIELLE
    Mommy. Her boyfriend. They make fun of me.
    I don't like being made fun of. Mommies aren't
    supposed to do that. Yours doesn't.

SHELLEY
    Maybe she's just teasing.

DANIELLE
No.

> *There is an awkward silence, followed by a peal of thunder.*

SHELLEY
It's really getting bad out there.

DANIELLE
I'm cold.

SHELLEY
Oh, my gosh, your clothes are still all wet. You must be freezing.

RALPH
Should I get a blanket?

SHELLEY
I'll get it, and I think I know where Mom put some of the clothes I outgrew. Maybe there's something in there that would fit you. I'll be back in a moment.

> *SHELLEY up and leaves the two sitting at the table.*

RALPH
When you draw, do you actually see the horse?

DANIELLE
Sort of. He kinda sees me, too.

RALPH
Wow.

DANIELLE
Sometimes he's there. Sometimes I have to call him.

RALPH
How do you call him?

DANIELLE
I do it with the colour. I just hold it up to the wall and, if I wish hard enough, he'll come.

RALPH picks up a pencil crayon and holds it up to the wall. He stands there for a moment.

RALPH
Nope, nothing.

DANIELLE
It's not that easy.

DANIELLE hesitates for a moment, then takes RALPH's pencil crayon and holds it up to the wall. She is motionless for a moment. Then her hand slowly begins to move as she begins to sketch the familiar pattern of THE HORSE on the wall. Her gestures have a familiar welcoming feel to them. She starts to smile as the image of THE HORSE begins to come through the wall. Alive once more, it goes to DANIELLE and once again dances with her in a gorgeous ballet.

Only this time, RALPH is watching. He is in her world and can see the three-dimensional horse and the dance they are doing together. At one point, THE HORSE comes close to RALPH,

*beckoning him to take part in their dance.
Hesitantly, RALPH lifts his hand, unsure of
what to do. They are about to touch when
DANIELLE notices this and shouts:*

DANIELLE
No!

*The mood and magic are broken and THE
HORSE disappears. RALPH is left in the kitchen
with his hand outstretched and an angry
DANIELLE standing in front of him.*

DANIELLE
No! It's my horse. Mine. You can't have him.

RALPH
Uh, I was …

DANIELLE
Mine. Please, I don't have anything else. Get
your own horse.

*At this moment, SHELLEY walks in with an
armful of clothes.*

SHELLEY
What's …?

*DANIELLE bolts out the door and out into the
rain. SHELLEY runs to the door.*

SHELLEY
Danielle! Danielle! Wait!

There is no response.

SHELLEY
What was that all about?

RALPH looks at his hand.

RALPH
I almost touched him.

Scene Nine

SHELLEY is sitting on the floor, an open box of clothes beside her. She is sorting the clothes. RALPH enters through the kitchen door, one side of his body covered in mud.

SHELLEY

What happened to you? Are you okay?

RALPH

Elsie Fiddler threw a beer bottle at me and I had to run as fast as I could to get out of range.

SHELLEY

You're kidding? Why?

RALPH

I just went there to see if Danielle had come home yet. I guess all those calls Mom made about trying to adopt her sort of made it back to Elsie. Told me to tell Mom to mind her own business or she'd come over here and punch her in the face. I think she'd been drinking.

SHELLEY

Well, considering she threw a beer bottle at you, you're probably right.

RALPH notices all the clothes.

RALPH
  What are you doing?

SHELLEY
  These are my old clothes. I was gonna give
  them to Danielle if she came to live with us. I
  think she'd look pretty in blue, don't you? I
  always wanted a sister.

RALPH
  It would have been kinda nice, huh? Having
  her here.

SHELLEY
  Why won't her mother let her come stay with
  us? Maybe if we told the police about her
  throwing that bottle at you, they'd change their
  minds and Danielle could …

RALPH
  Shelley, she can't. Mom tried. Elsie's her
  mother.

SHELLEY
  Some mother.

RALPH
  Maybe, but there's nothing we can do. We're
  just kids.

SHELLEY
  Ralph, there's gotta be something …

  *RALPH just shakes her head silently. She
  continues sorting the clothes in silence. RALPH*

tries to clean himself off. Then there's a loud
knocking at the door. It's WILLIAM.

SHELLEY
(*disappointed*) Oh.

RALPH
Haven't seen you in a while.

WILLIAM
Didn't think you wanted to.

SHELLEY
You got that right.

WILLIAM
Well, um, I guess I kinda got carried away the
other day. A little, maybe.

SHELLEY
No "little" about it, William.

WILLIAM
Well, look, I'm sorry. I blew up. I didn't mean
to. I don't know why I did. It just happened.

SHELLEY
You scared her.

WILLIAM
I know. I didn't mean to. Really. Just everybody
was talking about that stupid picture.

SHELLEY
She's missing, William. Nobody's seen her for
two days.

WILLIAM
  I know. I think I know where she is.

RALPH *&* SHELLEY
  You do?

WILLIAM
  Yeah, I was heading down to the lake. Was gonna spend the day out on our boat, been kinda bored since ... even brought my lunch for the day. So I was cutting across your backyard and through the woods. That's when I saw her in the doorway of the fort. You know, the one we hang out in during the summer.

SHELLEY
  Just behind the house.

WILLIAM
  I'm pretty sure it was her. Anyways, I thought you might like to know.

  WILLIAM turns to leave, but SHELLEY and RALPH prevent him, grabbing their coats and boots.

SHELLEY
  Not yet, William, you're coming with us.

  Delighted that he's part of the gang again, he brightens up.

WILLIAM
    Yeah, okay. Follow me.

       He dashes out the door with the other two
       following.

Scene Ten

*The location is the interior of a ramshackle fort
that has been put together over years by young
boys. Across the sloped and planked ceiling is the
drawing of THE HORSE, majestic and strong,
and perhaps bigger. In the corner of the fort on
the floor is DANIELLE, nestled happily in the
presence of the protective horse. It is a relationship
of love and security. She is singing or, more
accurately, mumbling, an inaudible song as she
basks in the warmth of THE HORSE. They are
playing a hand game.*

*Then from outside the fort, the voices of RALPH,
SHELLEY and WILLIAM are heard
approaching. Instantly, THE HORSE disengages
itself from the now-agitated DANIELLE and
re-enters the wall, only to disappear. Desperately,
DANIELLE tries to follow him into the wall but
fails. She has been left behind. The door of the
fort is opened and DANIELLE quickly hides
under a ratty old sleeping bag that has probably
been there for years.*

*She hides silently as the trio enters. They look
around and WILLIAM spots the huddled mass
in the corner. He silently points to her and
SHELLEY approaches, signalling the others to
stay behind.*

SHELLEY
Danielle? It's me, Shelley.

WILLIAM is the first to notice the image on the ceiling and nudges Ralph. No response from DANIELLE. SHELLEY sits beside her.

SHELLEY
Boy, it's cold in here. You can't be warm underneath that ratty thing. Come on, let's take you inside.

SHELLEY tries to remove the sleeping bag but DANIELLE won't let go. From across the room, RALPH speaks.

RALPH
Daniclle, I'm sorry.

WILLIAM
What have you got to be sorry for?

DANIELLE whimpers at the sound of WILLIAM's voice.

WILLIAM
Oh, um, Danielle, it's me, William. Well, I guess you know that. But I'm really sorry for all those things I said. I really like your horse. Honest.

DANIELLE peeks out from under the sleeping bag.

DANIELLE
Then why did you call him stupid?

WILLIAM
Um … because … I don't know, Danielle.

SHELLEY pulls the ratty sleeping bag away.
Slowly DANIELLE slides toward her.

WILLIAM
I guess I just wish I could draw like that.

SHELLEY
We've been looking all over the village for you.

DANIELLE
They were yelling again. All night. I don't
wanna live there anymore. I wanna stay with
you guys. I like your place.

SHELLEY
Did they hurt you or anything?

DANIELLE
No. Mommy's boyfriend got a job in Toronto.
We're moving there, but I don't want to go. I
wanna stay here. (*pause*) He scares me. Can I
stay with you guys? Please.

SHELLEY
Well, um, Danielle, we already thought of that.

DANIELLE
(*to RALPH*) I'll let you meet him. My horse.

SHELLEY
But your mom said no. We tried everything.
Really we did. Mom tried with the Children's

Aid Society, the band office, everything.
Nobody would help.

DANIELLE
I didn't think so.

RALPH
When are you going? To Toronto.

DANIELLE
Monday.

RALPH
So soon?

DANIELLE nods.

DANIELLE
What time is it?

WILLIAM
Almost lunchtime.

DANIELLE
I'm awful hungry.

*Realizing she hasn't eaten in two days,
SHELLEY and RALPH search through their
pockets for food of any kind. No luck until
WILLIAM pulls a paper lunch bag out of his
coat pocket.*

WILLIAM
Do you want my lunch?

*Nervous of WILLIAM, but very hungry, she
grabs it from his hand.*

DANIELLE
Thank you.

WILLIAM
It's just some sandwiches.

She proceeds to eat as fast as she can.

DANIELLE
Did my mother call looking for me? Was she worried about me?

SHELLEY
Yeah. She called. Of course she's worried. Wasn't she?

WILLIAM
Real worried.

RALPH
No, she didn't call.

DANIELLE
I didn't think so.

DANIELLE gets up to leave.

RALPH
Danielle, I'm sorry.

DANIELLE
That's okay. (*pause*) That was a pretty name you gave me. Girl Who Loved Her Horses. Pretty. I liked it.

RALPH
Way back when, Indian names said something about who you were or what you did. That's who I think you are.

DANIELLE
Thank you.

As she walks out the door, she has one final sentence for RALPH.

DANIELLE
I should have let you touch him. I should learn to share more. I'm sorry.

DANIELLE exits. The three remaining kids look miserable.

Scene Eleven

The now-older RALPH, SHELLEY and
WILLIAM enter the rundown city street where the
graffiti of THE HORSE is located.

SHELLEY
You know, to this day, every time I see a red
pickup, I can see her and that family of hers
driving by the school for the last time.

RALPH
I remember running to the window waving
goodbye.

WILLIAM
I spent that whole summer sitting in that fort
looking at the horse.

RALPH
There it is.

RALPH points to the half-covered horse on the
wall.

SHELLEY
Could be hers, but it doesn't look like the one I
remember.

RALPH
It's older, bigger, like us. It's gotta be her.

SHELLEY
Ralph, that was more than fifteen years ago.
People don't go around drawing horses on
walls for that long. That could be anybody.

RALPH
And how many people do you know who
suddenly stop and say, "Gee, I feel like drawing
a horse on a wall today for no particular
reason"?

SHELLEY
Maybe it's just wishful thinking, Ralph. Maybe
you'd just like to believe she's out there still
drawing that horse of hers.

WILLIAM
It's her.

SHELLEY
How do you know?

WILLIAM
That's the horse. I know it.

> WILLIAM approaches the wall and, like before,
> starts to pull at the flyers, grabbing handfuls and
> tossing them to the ground. First WILLIAM, then
> SHELLEY join him in a ripping frenzy. Soon,
> most of the drawing is free. They step back to
> appraise the bigger image.

SHELLEY
It's almost scary.

WILLIAM
Are you going to look for her?

RALPH
I don't know. Maybe she doesn't want to be
found.

WILLIAM
You should never bring horses to the city. They
don't belong here.

SHELLEY
So what now?

RALPH
I don't know.

SHELLEY
We can't just stand here looking at it all night.

WILLIAM
Let's go get something to eat. Maybe we can
come up with some ideas on how to find her.
We let her get away once. And that happened.

RALPH
(*to SHELLEY*) What do you say?

SHELLEY
I agree. And maybe we can stop somewhere and
pick up some black crayons.

RALPH
What for?

SHELLEY
  There's this kid in my class. I'm not going to
  give up again.

WILLIAM
  Let's go eat.

  *They turn and leave. RALPH lags behind, turns
  and approaches the drawing on the wall. He
  reaches out and touches the horse image for a
  moment.*

SHELLEY & WILLIAM
  Ralph!

RALPH
  Okay.

  He joins the others offstage.

  *From inside the wall on the empty stage, THE
  HORSE appears, angry and frustrated. Filled
  with rage, it dances and raises its arms to the
  wall, facing the audience, as if calling forth a
  power. The wall begins to radiate and pulsate,
  then the image of the horse painted on the wall
  begins to glow, solidify and take shape at the
  urging of THE HORSE. The picture of the horse
  gets brighter, stronger and more brilliant until the
  wall is seething in colour and presence. The
  magic and power of THE HORSE has returned.*

  *But unfortunately, nobody's there to see it. The
  lights go down.*

  The End.

Acknowledgements

As with so many things, a play is a collaborative effort, and the plays within these pages are no different. The hard work of many people went into making these works successful.

For their creativity, support and inspiration, I would like to thank Richard Greenblatt, Danielle Kappele, David Johnson, Larry Lewis, Kim Selody, Leslee Silverman (and the Manitoba Theatre for Young People), Andrey Tarasiuk (and Theatre Direct Canada), the cast and crew of both shows and my mother, for providing me the environment in which to be born.

And to everybody out there who put their two cents into these plays, and whom, for some reason, I have neglected to mention, your spirit lives strong in these words and I thank you from the bottom of my heart (and various other organs).

Ch'meegwetch!

—DREW HAYDEN TAYLOR